What Would Jesus Like For Christmas?

Kingdom Publishers

Copyright© Frances E Wilson 2025

All rights reserved. No part of this book may be reproduced in any form by photocopying or any electronic or mechanical means, including information storage or retrieval systems, without permission in writing from both the copyright owner and the publisher of the book. The right of Frances E Wilson to be identified as the author of this work has been asserted by her in accordance with the Copyright, Designs, and Patents Act 1988 and any subsequent amendments thereto.

A catalogue record for this book is available from the British Library.

All Scripture quotations have been taken from The Passion Translation (*unless stated*) version of the Bible.

ISBN: 978-1-916801-38-7

1st Edition 2025 by Kingdom Publishers, London, UK.

You can purchase copies of this book from any leading bookstore or at:
www.kingdompublishers.co.uk

Dedication

In loving memory of Judith (Judy) Faulkner – the greatest friend, co-worker and encourager God could have possibly given me.

Thank you Judy and thank you God.

Grateful Thanks

My very grateful thanks go to Lorna Beedham for all her encouragement to get this book finished and for correcting all my poor punctuation and giving really helpful suggestions. Bless you, I'm so privileged to have you as a friend.

My equally grateful thanks go to Peter, who runs the most amazing IT distance rescue service for novices like me, actually just for me, as I really haven't a clue. Your patience, grace and determination to find a way, where there seems to be no way, have been outstanding. God bless you beyond your greatest dreams. Thank you so much for being a real friend.

Acknowledgements

Scripture quotations are from The Passion Translation unless otherwise stated – Scriptures marked NIV are from the New International Version, AMP are from the Amplified version. AMPC are from the Amplified Bible, Classic Edition.

Emphasis within Scripture is the author's own.

All pronouns referring to the Father, Son, and Holy Spirit are capitalised and may differ from some Bible publishers' style, and the name of satan and related names are not capitalised, as we choose not to acknowledge him, even to the point of violating grammatical rules.

The words of 'As with gladness..' by W.C.Dix are taken from Golden Bells Hymns for Young People. Second edition. 1925/6

Endorsement

As you read this book you will get to know the prayerful and 'set apart' woman of God Fran Wilson is. She has a heart to walk closely with God and help others to do the same. If you struggle with prayer you will find the words you need in the prayers she has written. If you find it hard to get to an intimate place with God let Fran's conversations with God take you there. If you have lost your adoration for, gratitude to and expectation of God let her words rekindle them within you. And once you have done that, follow the characters of the Christmas Story through their journeys of adoration, gratitude and expectation and collect your own nuggets of gold from their experiences of God the Father, Son and Holy Spirit. This is a book that shows God is about relationship with all people including you. I would encourage you to sit quietly and let Fran's words bring you into the presence of the Father so that you too can give Him all your adoration, gratitude and expectation.

Lorna Beedham, publisher poet and trustee of
Life Church Bedworth

Contents

What would bring You joy? — 13
The gift of Adoration — 15
Introduction — 16

Part 1 — 19 - 91
    Adoration – for Who God Is — 20
    The Amazing Creator — 22
    The Prolific Designer — 23
    Your Artistic Spontaneity — 25
    The Servant — 26
    The Wonderful Counsellor — 28
    The Mighty God — 30
    The Everlasting Father — 32
    The Prince of Peace — 33
What is Gratitude? — 39
The Gift of Gratitude — 42
The Attitude of Gratitude — 47
That You are:
    My Life — 47
    My Provider — 52
    My Healer — 54

My Husband	56
My Protector, Shelter and Refuge	57
My Director	64
My Intercessor	67
My Comforter	76
My Salvation / Saviour / Redeemer	79
Expectancy:	86

Part 2   95 - 173

The Adoration, Gratitude and Expectation of:	
Zechariah	96
Elisabeth	109
Mary and Joseph	114
The Shepherds	131
Simeon	142
Anna	146
The Wise Men	151
Epilogue	171

'Lord what would bring You the greatest JOY this Christmas from me, from us?'

'Do I have any gifts I can bring You? Give You?'

'I know You don't *need* anything but is there anything You would enjoy?'

'Do I hear You whisper' -
    "Your time and your company?"

"Your time and your company and then you can give Me the gift I will treasure above all."

"I would really like

The Gift

of

Your AGE."

'The Gift of My Age?'

"Yes Please, the gift of the

Adoration,

Gratitude,

Expectation

of your heart."

Introduction

One Christmas Day, feeling a mixture of 'disturbed' and 'sad' I went to my tiny bedroom – 5ft 10ins by 8ft - and fell on my knees at the side of the 2ft wide bed, a thing I rarely did for fear of hitting my head painfully on the wall, and I quietly, but earnestly, asked,

'Jesus, what would YOU like for Christmas?'

I was so sad and disturbed that Jesus was being more and more left out of, even obliterated from Christmas in the shops, in advertising, in schools, in family life and even among Christians.

Although my question was very sincere I didn't particularly expect an answer, though I genuinely wanted one. I just knelt there, with my head on the duvet, and in the silence came a very clear response :

"I would like the gift of your Age!"

'You what?'

"I would like the gift of your Age!"

'What do You mean Lord? I'm 67 so what does *that* mean?'

And then, in my mind, I saw the word AGE written as an acrostic :

A doration,

G ratitude, and

E xpectancy.

So Jesus was saying to me "I would like the gift of your Adoration, Gratitude and Expectancy". It was nothing to do with my physical age and this was a gift that He didn't just want for Christmas, or on special days, but all year round. Wow! Then my heart and mind began to ponder all the different characters in the original Christmas story and to consider their differing levels of Adoration, Gratitude and Expectancy as they became involved.

First of all I had to determine what these 3 qualities really were.

Secondly, how the Christmas characters (who are in chronological order of appearance in this book) exhibited any or all of these 3 qualities and if their levels increased or decreased as their story unfolded.

Thirdly, I was challenged to apply what I discovered to my own life and to question what 'size' gift I am giving to Jesus day by day.

My hope and prayer is that you will find it as eye-opening and challenging as I have - maybe even more so - as you allow the Holy Spirit to apply Jesus' request for your A
G
E to your own personal daily walk with our amazing God. He chose to come to earth, that first Christmas, as a tiny Babe in order to introduce us to our Heavenly Father and to provide the only way for us to enjoy His presence and company for all of eternity. He did this by dying on the Cross and paying the ultimate penalty for all our sins and shortcomings if we will accept His solution.

There are many questions through the book for us to ponder and answer but it's so important that we quietly ask the Holy Spirit to show us what our real answers should be and not fool ourselves by over, or under, estimating where we are really at.

If the Holy Spirit shows you more about this gift that Jesus would like from you than is already written here, it would be lovely to hear from you if you want to share.

May God's mercy, peace and love

cascade over you!'

Jude 1:2

Part 1

So let's start by considering what

Adoration of God

really looks like.

This is not a book to be rushed through. It's a book to enter into, to open our hearts as well as our minds and to listen to what Almighty God wants to share with us as we ponder each amazing aspect as He reveals Himself to us in Jesus and in the Bible, through the working of the Holy Spirit.

So you are invited to take time, make notes so you can ponder again and again the revelations that come to you.

Adoration - for Who God Is.

Adoration = Worshipping with fervent love from the heart, the mind, the body, the soul and spirit.

Worshipping with - all my deepest heart.

                                           - profound love and regard.

                                           - fervent and devoted love.

                                           - really deep intensity.

Psalm 2:10 Message

'Worship God in adoring embrace.'

Real adoration takes time. We can't adore something or someone with a fleeting glance or a nod of our head.

We have to ponder, mull over, spend time contemplating in order to adore. It's not a vague gooey feeling; it's direct and intentional.

We should be able to say to God,

> You are : The Great Creator
> > and I adore You for it.
>
> : The most prolific Designer
> > and I adore You for it.
>
> : The most spontaneous Artist
> > and I adore You for it.
>
> : The Servant of all who will receive Your service
> > and I adore You for it.
>
> : The Wonderful Counsellor
> > and I adore You.
>
> : The Mighty God
> > and I adore You.
>
> : The Everlasting Father
> > and I adore You.
>
> : The Prince of Peace
> > and I adore You.

God, You are the great, amazing Creator.

Unlike all other creators You created something out of nothing; You created everything out of nothing.

Everything You created was perfect and fitted in perfectly with everything else You created.

The span of Your creativity is just way beyond our ken. Lord, thousands of years later man is still trying to find out more about Your creation and how it was created. Yet as the great Creator You subjected Yourself to Your Creation and became a tiny babe and lived as a part of Your creation.

Lord, a potter can't become part of a pot; a gardener can't become part of a garden; a mathematician can't become a formula; but YOU, because You are Almighty God, could become part of Your creation and not only could, but did. You chose to endure the massive indignity and rejection by Your very own creation while You were in it.

A Prayer: Lord, I'm so sorry - You've always been rejected by the human part of Your creation from Adam and Eve onwards and now, in spite of Calvary when You were very publicly rejected, along with all You did for us, You are still rejected massively today and Lord so much of that rejection comes from Your Church.

Oh Lord please show me / us how to really repent of rejecting You in any way and then to receive You in every way.

Lord, I adore You for Your amazing creation – wherever I go there is always more to see, to hear, to feel, to smell and to taste.

Thank You SO much for being such a Creator.

Amen.

Lord, You are the most prolific Designer.

Lord how many snowflakes have You designed since snow first fell and each one is different?

Lord how many flowers of any species have You designed and each one is different?

Lord how many people have You designed through the ages and none are the same, not even identical twins are exactly the same? Everyone is individually designed by You.-Yes we know the genes of the parents have a part to play etc. but Lord, You designed the 'system' that would cause every person to be unique and special. Such is Your amazing ability to design.

Lord, You also designed a completely unsinkable boat to house the most enormous zoo the world has ever known.

And Lord, I adore You because You designed the most beautiful, practical, portable Church – the Tabernacle. You designed the place for Your people to meet with You, even in the middle of the wilderness, where every need was met for them to come into Your so holy Presence.

Lord, I adore You because You have entrusted some of Your design ability to humans. That was a very risky thing to do but You chose to do so knowing that some would design for good and others for evil. But You chose to put part of Your divinity in each of us.

You could have been an amazing designer without being a creator but You are both and spontaneous with it.

A Prayer:

Dear Lord, I adore You and marvel that You have put some of Your attributes in me – in little diddy me – and I ask Your forgiveness for the many times and ways I have misused these gifts. I ask that from now on, by the enabling of the Holy Spirit, all that I design, be it a multi-million pound complex or a meal for one, I will do it for Your glory and with You very clearly in my heart and mind.

I fervently love You because You have never stopped creating and You also recreate and make things new where damage has been done by people or by illness if we will let You.

Amen.

Lord, I adore Your artistic spontaneity.

Sunsets, sunrises, clouds! Every day You paint new pictures in the skies. We never know exactly how they'll be but this we know, they'll always be new.

Thank You Lord.

Thank You Lord that Your mercies are always new, - every morning, not just occasionally if I've been especially good, but *every* morning.

A Prayer :

Oh Holy Spirit please awaken my spirit to the spontaneity of Jesus so that I receive the gentle, all-embracing hugs and hear the whisper that says, "Don't be afraid; I am with you." That says, "I know your hurt and heartache but trust Me. I have an amazing plan for you if you will let Me do it My way for you – My spontaneous way - not your calculated way."

Oh Lord, thank You. Thank You that You do have a perfect plan for me. I open myself up to Your spontaneity with a wee bit of excitement, if trepidation, because You are the Almighty, spontaneous Designer and Creator and, in theory, I know that You are completely trustworthy and amazingly loving. Please help me believe it and give You free reign to lead me however and wherever You would like.

Amen.

Lord, I adore You for being the Servant of all who will receive Your service.

Jesus, You said, speaking of Yourself, "The Son of man did not come expecting to be served but to serve" Matthew 20:28

This is amazing! - You have come to serve me! You do not need my help or assistance at all - and I adore You for that and for Your completeness. But in that completeness, Your desire is to serve me as I seek to be and do what You have lovingly planned for me to be and do.

That You, Almighty God, should have the slightest desire to serve little, diddy, insignificant me is just mind-blowing, but it's true. Please help me to understand and take on board, in my life, the implications of this.

Jesus 'You came not to be served but to serve and give Your life a ransom for many'. Matthew 20:28 RSV

You have paid the price in full for our Salvation. The price of Your life was considered to be the price of a slave, 30 pieces of silver. Not only have You Redeemed us (bought us back) and paid the price for our personal salvation but You continue to redeem every situation that we are in by serving us. You enable and equip us to walk / live through every day as Sons and Daughters of the King of Kings who You have called to serve the rest of humanity on Your behalf.

A Prayer :

Lord, help me not to react like Peter first did when You went to wash his feet. John 13v3-10. Humbly I choose to receive Your service into my life each day – I can't do anything of lasting value unless I do.

    I thank You so much for the priceless privilege of being served by the Almighty God and ask that I may always be willing to receive the service that You see I need so that in time I may, in turn, give the service that You see others need.

    Dear Holy Spirit, please will You teach me how to receive this amazing service with adoration and gratitude.

Amen.

God, You are the Wonderful Counsellor and I adore You for that.

Lord, not only are You a 'good' Counsellor but You are a *wonderful* one. - Not only do You have wise counsel to give in any and every situation to any and every person who will receive it, but You have a wonderful way of sharing, imparting the counsel that we need and You know how we can receive it and when.

Lord, Your counsel is very different from the world's. The world says 'Focus on the problem and get it sorted no matter what it does to others'. You say "Focus on Me and together we will sort it in a while, but first focus on Me."

Your counsel is "Delight Yourself in Me and I will give you the desires of your heart. Delight in the fact that I am your WONDERFUL counsellor – yes, I am WONDER FULL. You have only caught a tiny glimpse of the signs and wonders - miracles that I have done, am doing and will do. Open your heart and mind to a state of expectancy, expecting to see Me do many mighty miracles. There is so much in Me that you have not yet understood, experienced or enjoyed and I want you to, not just for My sake, but for yours too, because as you delight in Me you will come to realise and enjoy My delight in you."

Lord, Your Word is SO full of wonderful counsel and I adore You for it :

> Matthew 11:28 NKJV- 'Come unto Me all you who labour and are heavy ladened'

Matthew 6:33 KJV- 'Seek ye first the kingdom of heaven..'

Proverbs 3:5-6 KJV- 'Trust in the Lord with all of your heart and lean not unto your own understanding....'

Colossians 3:2 NIV - 'Set your mind on the things that are above.'

A Prayer :

Dear Lord, You have given me so much wonder-full written counsel. Please help me every day to seek Your counsel and then to do it so that my life will bring You glory and, both You and I, joy.

Amen.

Lord, You are..... The Mighty God.

You are indeed the ALL Mighty God. There is only one thing You cannot do and that is fail. You cannot fail because You are SO mighty.

Your power is totally beyond anyone's calculation.

Your power is so immense that You only had to *speak* a word and the world was made, the raging storm was immediately abated, leprosy vanished, the lame walked and the dead were raised. - You are so mighty that You don't have to heave or push or shove or shout, just a word from You displays Your omnipotence.

Because You are so mighty You can afford to be so loving, so gentle, so caring because no-one or nothing can take Your power from You.

You are Your power. It's not something You have developed over time – Your power is eternal and undilutable and because Your power is You and You are All-Mighty, You are always in control of Your power.

Your power is such that when the devil tempted You in the desert You answered him each time with Your own Word and he had to turn tail. And on the Cross You had the last Word, "It is finished," demonstrating that You are indeed the Mighty God.

A Prayer :

Oh Jesus, I rejoice that You are indeed the ALL Mighty God. Please forgive me that so often I forget :

> The might of Your power to save,
>> The might of Your power to keep,
>>> The might of Your power to protect
>>>> and so I fear,
>>> I doubt,
>>>> I am anxious
>>>>> and try to do things in my own strength.
>>>> Please forgive me Lord.

May I choose to trust Your Omnipotence each day and walk closely in Your shadow adoring You as we walk together.

Amen.

God You are …… the Everlasting Father and I adore you

Jesus, You said quite clearly John 10:30 NIV "I and My Father are one."

You have revealed the Everlasting Father to us, and there will never come a time in our lives when He will cease to be our Father. Lord, an earthly father may abandon or desert us or die prematurely but because You are the EVERLASTING Father You never will, You can't. Your Father heart is always beating for us whether we acknowledge You as our Father or not.

I adore You because You never make mistakes in Your parenting of us. Please forgive me that I have often abused Your parenting – ignored Your wisdom, Your chiding, Your correcting, Your directions and blame You for what has resulted; for the consequences.

I love You deeply for always receiving me back when I've stubbornly gone my own way, when I've squandered Your gifts to me of time, money, energy and love.

A Prayer :

Oh Holy Spirit, will You please enable me to use all that Father has given me, through Jesus, wisely, joyfully and effectively so that They get all the glory.

Amen.

God You are ...... the Prince of Peace

Jesus You say in John 14:27 RSV "MY peace I give unto you .. Not as the world gives...."

The world is trying to get external peace – hence peace talks, treaties, truces etc. but You give internal peace – peace which passes *all* understanding, peace which makes us ask the question 'Where did that come from?' because all around war, chaos, storms are raging at one level or another.

Lord, You demonstrated Your peace so many times. Such as when You slept in the boat in the midst of the storm; when You showed no signs of panic when faced with 4000 / 5000 plus hungry people; or the violent demoniac; or Judas' angry mob in the Garden; or the Sanhedrin at Your trial.

Lord, what mechanism have You given us for *receiving* Your peace? You've given it so the problem must be with our receiving it. Lord, what is our receiver?

Is it real trust? Trust that You are completely reliable, completely able to cope / deal with any and every situation, and that we don't have to strive, struggle, or manipulate in order to get through?

Because Your peace 'passes understanding' we don't have to know how things, situations, people are going to work out but we do have to trust that You know. So often how You work things out is way beyond our understanding, because 'Your ways are NOT our ways' Isaiah 55:8 RSV but we need to trust You that Your ways *are* the best and therefore we can receive Your peace.

Does lack of *real* peace

=

lack of *real* trust?

Does *real* trust

=

real peace?

Peace that 'passes understanding' -

that bypasses understanding where necessary.

Lord the opposite of peace is anger, bitterness, resentment, damaged pride etc. - all these things are in the mind. That's where they grow and fester and then trespass into our hearts and have a field day.

You give peace that passes our current understanding, that gives a new mindset, that views things through different 'glasses;' but we have to be willing to put them on and keep them on.

Peace is a top-to-toe garment. When we don't have Your peace which passes understanding we won't be wearing the 'shoes of the Gospel of peace'. We'll have hobnail boots on which trample on others and make a lot of disturbing noise while causing much damage.

These shoes of the Gospel of peace are designed so the wearer can walk safely, sure-footed, quietly, unobtrusively, on any terrain.

Just as we have to choose to receive the mindset of God's peace so we have to choose and make the effort to 'put on' the shoes of the 'Gospel of peace.' Shoes don't just appear on our feet we have to choose which shoes to put on and then we have to actually put them on. Just choosing isn't enough, we have to act as well.

In order to put on the shoes of the Gospel of peace we have to take off all other shoes – we can't wear two pairs at a time.

We may wake up with the shoes of despair or anger on but we have to choose to take them off; throw them in the 'bin' (not taking them out later); and put on the shoes of the Gospel of peace.

Lord, because You are the Prince of Peace and we are part of Your Royal Household all that we need is wonderfully provided – both 'glasses' and 'shoes' – our responsibility is to put them on; keep them clean; and keep them on. These glasses and shoes are even to be kept on while sleeping – there is NO need, in fact it is detrimental, to take them off.

In Isaiah 26:4 NKJV You have promised that "You will keep him in perfect peace whose mind is stayed on You because he trusts in You"

- whose mind is fixed -

    securely anchored to,

        centred on You.

Prince of Peace, You give Your peace to those whose *mind* is *fixed* on You, not to a double minded person, for they cannot receive Your peace – it has nowhere to land because the mind is vacillating and unstable.

In Colossians 1:2 NIV You tell us to 'set your minds on the things above, not on the things that are on earth.'

In Colossians 3:15 AMPC it says 'Let the peace of Christ rule / umpire in your hearts' not just sometimes but continually – there is never ½ time or time out when we don't need Jesus umpiring in our minds and hearts.

Lord we need You as umpire, coach, manager and owner and then we will walk in Your path of peace.

A Prayer :

Lord Jesus, thank You that You are the Prince of Peace – You are in charge of peace and You have a totally unlimited supply of it which You delight to give and share with all who will fix their minds on You. Indeed, thinking about You brings peace to our troubled minds if we choose to trust You and if we put on the shoes of the Gospel of peace and walk quietly through the storms and uncertainties.

Holy Spirit, please help me to stop whinging about my lot and prompt me to re-fix my eyes, my mind and my heart on Jesus the Prince of Peace whenever I begin to lose focus.

May I become more and more responsive to Your promptings day by day.

Amen.

You may want to add other reasons why you adore our amazing God. Please do.

~ For your thoughts ~

~ For your thoughts ~

Gratitude

Let's consider what Gratitude is,

    and why we have so much to be

        grateful to God for.

Gratitude

    for what God has done,

        for what God is doing,

            for what God will do &

              who He is for me.

Gratitude is an attitude of

    real,

        deep,

            lasting,

                thankfulness.

Gratitude is an attitude of the heart

            as well as the mind.

Gratitude is not just sending a 'thank you' letter because we know we should, though that is good, or even sending an annual 'thank you' on the anniversary of when the gift was given, that may be good too, but it's having a continuously grateful heart that will bring much joy to the giver and a beautiful attitude in the receiver.

Our depth of gratitude will depend on how desperately we were/are in need of the gift, or how much we longed for it. For example, if a very wealthy Uncle Walter gives you an ordinary box of chocolates for Christmas you will no doubt enjoy them and hopefully write a 'thank you' letter, but you will forget about the gift soon after it's contents have been consumed. However, if when you so badly needed it he, or maybe someone you don't even know, gave you one of their kidneys because yours has failed to function properly and you are struggling to survive, you would do more than write a thank you letter, even annually. Every time you were able to enjoy life to the full your heart, as well as your mind, would be so overflowing with gratitude. Surely your thankfulness would last for the rest of your life!

You would live in an 'Attitude of Gratitude' for the new life you had been given and all the possibilities that came with the gift.

Real gratitude is on-going, - not just a quick 'thank you'.

It takes time to remember the enormous generosity of God. It's not just an occasional gooey feeling; or doffing our cap as we pass by.

Gratitude is real and intentional, as well as sometimes spontaneous, in it's out-working.

The Gift of Gratitude.

God, You have : Saved me from the penalty of my sin,

                         and I'm so grateful.

: Redeemed me - paid the ransom price for my life,

                         and I'm so grateful.

: Delivered me from my addiction to my sin,

                         and I'm so grateful.

: Provided me with all I need in every part of my life,

                         and I'm so grateful.

: Guided me through my life,

                         and I'm so grateful.

: Healed me from sickness, abuse & deprivation,

                         and I'm so grateful.

: Given me Your precious Word,

                         and I'm so grateful.

: Given me Your empowering Holy Spirit,

                         and I'm so grateful.

: Given me Your peace that passes understanding,

                         and I'm so grateful.

: Given me Your joy to make me strong,

                         and I'm so grateful.

In Psalm 50:23 the psalmist speaks God's words when he says;-

"The life that pleases Me is a life lived in the

Gratitude of Grace;

always choosing to walk with Me in what is right."

Grace can be defined as : 'God's unmerited favour'.

A Prayer :

'Oh dear holy Trinity, may I always live consciously with an attitude of real thankfulness for all that You have done for me; are doing; and will do in the future. I don't deserve Your favour at all but am so grateful that You delight to shower me with Your unmerited favour so long as I walk close to You in glad obedience day by day. Oh! What amazing blessings You choose to give me. Thank you so much.

Amen.

Rejoice!

Real Gratitude is an attribute negatives and sin *cannot* co-habit with.

Gratitude for –

    what You've done,

        what You are doing and

            what You will do, and

                who You are for me.

Gratitude

    =

        Thanking with deep, heart-felt, genuine, on-going thankfulness.

The Gift of Gratitude.

Real Gratitude takes time to enjoy what we are grateful for.

Thank You dear God that You are :

>My Life,
>>I'm so grateful.
>
>My Provider,
>>I'm so grateful.
>
>My Healer,
>>I'm so grateful.
>
>My Husband,
>>I'm so grateful.
>
>My Protector / Shelter / Refuge,
>>I'm so grateful.
>
>My Director,
>>I'm so grateful.
>
>My Intercessor
>>I'm so grateful.
>
>My Comforter,
>>I'm so grateful.
>
>My Salvation / Redeemer / Saviour,
>>I'm so grateful.

Gratitude begets generosity and generosity begets increased genuine Gratitude.

The more grateful we are the more we will have to be grateful for.

God *loves* a cheerful giver and that applies to giving Gratitude too. 2 Corinthians 9:7 KJV.

Gratitude is an attitude,

It is a beautiful attribute.

In Acts 5:41 the early Church were thankful that they were considered worthy to suffer disgrace for the name of Jesus.

They had an attitude of Gratitude.

Lord, when is physical suffering something that we should accept with gratitude that we are counted worthy to bear it for the name of Christ, be it illness or persecution and when is it something that we should refuse / resist as coming totally from the enemy?

I have a choice with any suffering that is not self-inflicted, be it great or small, physical or emotional, to have an attitude of Gratitude that Father knows that with the Holy Spirit's enabling I can cope with it, even rejoice in it and bring honour to His name. Either the test becomes a sweet testimony, or I can be angry and shout 'Why me?' and try and deal with it in my own strength and bring dishonour to His beautiful name.

The Attitude of Gratitude

I'm so grateful that You are …….

My LIFE.

Paul said in Galatians 2:20 'The life which I now live in the flesh I live by the faith of the Son of God Who loved me and gave Himself for me.'

Jesus said in John 10:10 "I am come that you may have life and have it more abundantly."

You are my life both physically and spiritually.

You keep me breathing on both levels.

Life -   We are all 'Lifers' and there are only 2 choices -

- A life of freedom in Christ -

- Or a life of bondage without Christ.

The latter may look fine for a long while but the end is eternity without Christ which means eternity with satan. There are NO alternatives.

We are not condemned to one or the other – the choice is ours but if we don't choose Life in Christ we have already chosen the alternative. We cannot live with one foot in each camp – it doesn't work, it's all or nothing either way. If we really choose Life in Christ, the Holy Spirit will come and enable us day by day to enter into all that life in Christ means. He will come and work in our hearts and minds encouraging us, prompting us to receive new ways of thinking, new desires, new goals, new motives, new focus. So long as we receive His nudges, the Holy Spirit will continually 'upgrade' our life in Christ.

In order to live a healthy physical life we have to take daily time out to 1) Eat and digest good food: 2) to exercise: and 3) to sleep, then we can live the rest of the day to the full.

In order to live a healthy spiritual life we have to take daily time out to: 1) Eat and digest 'good food' - to study, to ponder, to mull over part of the Word of God and take it into our lives – it's no good if we look at it but leave it on the plate. (Suggestion for those who live / eat alone that when you have a physical meal you also have a spiritual one too).

2) 'Exercise' our faith in prayer and intercession – standing in the gap for others – not on a treadmill or static bike but on a cross-country, cross-continent, cross-global run to those places that the Holy Spirit brings to our attention.

3) 'Sleep'- to be silent and still in His presence so that He can share some of His secrets, passions and desires with us in whatever way He chooses to reveal them but also that We – He and I – can just enjoy each others' company.

Do I come into His presence to get what I want for myself and even for others or to enjoy His company?

Yes Lord, You want to enjoy my time in Your company on a regular but special basis, not just occasionally.

A Prayer :

    I am so grateful that YOU are my life. May I live YOU to the full, not just sometimes but continuously.

    Lord, it's not about improving my existence it's about Your Holy Spirit transforming it – having NEW life in Christ not the old one patched up.

    Thank You for the great exchange You are offering me – You will take my completely inferior, often messed up life and give me Your glorious, whole, exciting life not just for a day but for eternity. I choose to accept Your amazing offer and ask You Holy Spirit to come and work it out in my whole being.

Amen.

Lord it says in Your Word- in fact You said it Yourself

John 14:6

"I am THE way,   THE truth,   THE life..."

You are THE Life.

You are not just 'Life' but You are

THE Life.

There is no *real* Life apart from You.

Adam and Eve had real life to begin with – eternal life. You didn't intend them to die but by disobeying Your one command they chose death. Yes, they caused physical death to come into the world.

Because of their disobedience they lost the joy of companionship with Creator God Whom they were used to talking and walking with in the cool of the day. They lost that LIFE relationship.

Because of their disobedience they died to peace and lived in fear – they hid themselves.

They died to enjoying each other; instead they blamed each other.

They died to controlling creation with God-given authority to having to work hard to control the weeds etc. with their own authority.

Physical death took many years to happen but spiritual death was instant.

Lord, thank You that You are THE Life and when we come to You in true repentance You give us spiritual Life in an instant.

You have the power and delight to reverse our spiritual death – which we were physically born into – and give us THE Life and You give it abundantly and You want us to receive it abundantly day by day.

You are THE way to true Life,

You are THE true way to / of Life.

Yes we live physically in a fallen world but You want us to enjoy that newness of Life and live in, and from, a heavenly perspective while here on earth :

Enjoying Your company day by day.

Enjoying each others' company day by day,

Living in the peace which passes understanding and not in fear.

Holy Spirit, help us to receive it - the newness of Life in Christ Jesus.

Living in Truth and not in deceit – Holy Spirit, help us to receive it.

Living in Delight and not in disappointment – Holy Spirit, help us to receive it.

Living in Joy and not in grief – Holy Spirit, help us to receive it.

Living in Comfort and not in distress – Holy Spirit, help us to receive it.

Living in gentle authority and not in manipulative, controlling power – Holy Spirit, help us to receive it.

Living in Humility and not in pride – Holy Spirit, help us to receive it.

Living in Creativeness and not in destruction – Holy Spirit, help us to receive the newness of Life that Jesus alone offers.

A Prayer :

Oh Lord Jesus, I am SO grateful that You came and died so that I could die with You and rise with You to live in the newness of Life, the abundant Life that You offer. I choose to accept Your amazing offer for the rest of my existence, now and throughout eternity.

Amen.

I'm so grateful that You are ……..

My PROVIDER.

You have provided, are providing and have promised to provide all that I have needed, am needing and ever will need.

Philippians 4:19 NIV says 'my God will meet all your needs according to His riches in glory in Christ Jesus.'

There is NO shortage of supplies!

My Provider of Peace – "I leave the gift of peace with you – My peace, not the kind of fragile peace given by the world, but My perfect peace. Don't yield to fear or be troubled in your hearts – instead be courageous."

John 14:27

My Provider of Power and Love – 'For God did not give us a spirit of timidity or cowardice or fear, but He has given us a spirit of power and of love and of sound judgement and personal discipline, abilities that result in a calm, well-balanced mind and self-control.'

2 Timothy 1:7 AMP

My Provider of a Way of Escape - '….when you are tempted He will also provide a way out so that you can endure it.'

1 Corinthians 10:13 NIV

My Provider of Food - 'The Lord is my shepherd, I lack nothing. He makes me lie down in green pastures, He leads me beside quiet waters, He refreshes my soul. …. You prepare a table before me in the presence of my enemies…..'

Psalm 23:1-3,5 NIV

My Provider of Grace – 'My grace is always more than enough for you, and my power finds its full expression through your weakness.'

2 Corinthians 12:9

My Provider of Rest - "Come to Me, all you who are weary and burdened and I will give you rest …"

Matthew 11:28 NIV

My Provider of a new heart and a new spirit – "I will give you a new heart and put a new spirit in you; I will remove from you your heart of stone and give you a heart of flesh."

Ezekiel 36:26 NIV

My Provider of beauty, joy and praise – "The Lord has sent Me to …… provide for those who grieve … a crown of beauty instead of ashes, the oil of joy instead of mourning and a garment of praise instead of the spirit of despair."

Isaiah 61:3 NIV

A Prayer :

Lord Jesus, I'm so grateful that I can trust You to provide for me day by day, You haven't promised to supply all I want, but You have promised to supply all I need. May I always sit at the bountiful table You have provide for me, even in the presence of my enemies, and not at their table of doubt, despair, fear, dismay or disbelief, and enjoy, to the full, Your presence and Your bounteous provision. Thank you that there is NO lack of provision on Your part, please increase my ability to receive all You have provided for me.

Amen!

I'm so grateful that You are …….

My HEALER.

It is so wonderful to know that You are ALL-Mighty God and there is no person, situation, relationship that You cannot heal if we are willing to cooperate with You. Often You want to heal our hearts and minds before our bodies. You want to heal our prejudices, our offences about what others have done to us or others, be it real or imaginary, and our assumptions that whatever needs healing will just keep reoccurring because it has for so long.

There is NO limit to your ability to heal.

But, just as in 2 Chronicles 12:9 NIV, You sometimes put a condition on the healing taking place. You said, "IF My people, who are called by My name, will humble themselves *and* pray *and* seek My face *and* turn from their wicked ways, THEN I *will* hear from heaven, and I *will* forgive their sin and *will* heal their land."

In Psalm 30:2-3 David said, 'O Lord, my healing God, I cried out for a miracle and you healed me! You brought me back from the brink of death.' - He had to cry out before God healed him.

In Psalm 103 David delights, revels in what God has done for him. In v2-3 he says, 'How could I ever forget the miracles of kindness You've done for me? You kissed my heart with forgiveness, in spite of all I've done. You've healed me inside and out from every disease.' Enjoy the whole Psalm, especially in the TPT version: God wants to do the same for each one of us.

Psalm 107:19-20 says, 'Then we cried out, 'Lord, help us! Rescue us!' And He did! God spoke the words "Be healed" and we were healed and delivered from death's door.'

This is our Healer God.

Psalm 147:3,5 says about our healing-God, 'He heals the wounds of every shattered heart.... How great is our God! There's absolutely nothing His power cannot accomplish, and He has infinite understanding of everything.'

In 1 Peter 2:24, speaking of Jesus, Peter says, 'He Himself carried our sins in His body on the cross so that we would be dead to sin and alive for righteousness. Our instant healing flowed from His wounding.'

In Luke 4:18 Jesus quotes from Isaiah 61:1-3. NIV

'The Spirit of the Sovereign Lord is upon me, 'because :'

He has anointed Me to proclaim good news to the poor.

He has sent Me to bind up the broken-hearted,

To proclaim freedom for the captives, and

Release from darkness the prisoners,

To proclaim the year of the Lord's favour and the day of vengeance of our God,

To comfort all who mourn and provide for those who grieve in Zion -

To bestow on them a crown of beauty instead of ashes,

The oil of joy instead of mourning, and

The garment of praise instead of a spirit of despair.'

God's healing embraces every aspect of a human's life be it personal, corporate, national, or international, political, ethical, environmental, physical, emotional, mental, spiritual, lifestyle, intellectual, trauma, abuse or rejection.

'By His stripes we are healed' Isaiah 53:5

I'm so grateful that You are ....

My HUSBAND

Isaiah 54 : 5-6 says You, God are my maker and yet you also want to be my HUSBAND – WOW! - even though you know all my faults and failings.

In Bible times a good husband would expend much energy and thought over how to build up his wife. He would not primarily be thinking about how or whether she is serving him, he'd be focused on what he can do for her. A biblical husband was an initiating husband.

Oh the joy of saying 'I DO' to Yahweh, the Commander of Angel Armies, to our Kinsman-Redeemer, the Holy One of Israel, the Mighty God of all the earth not just once at the beginning of our relationship but continually, day by day.

Suggestion – read the book of Ruth in the Old Testament.

May we follow Ruth's example and prostrate ourselves at the feet of Jesus and enjoy all He longs to do for us personally.

A Prayer – Dear Jesus, I am amazed that You want me as Your wife and I'm so grateful that Your desire is to build me up, to share Your thoughts and secrets with me so that we – You and I – can work in partnership to bring to birth all that is in Your heart for those You've put me amongst.

May my life's desire be to know You more intimately each day and to bring You much joy as I seek to hear and follow Your slightest whisper, knowing that of myself I can do nothing of eternal significance but that with You all things are possible.

Amen.

I'm so grateful that you are ………..

My PROTECTOR, SHELTER & REFUGE

In Psalm 144:1-2 David says, 'There is only one strong, safe and secure place for me; it's in God alone and I love Him! He's the one Who gives me strength and skill for the battle. He's my Shelter of Love and my Fortress of Faith, Who wraps Himself around me as a secure Shield. I hide myself in the one Who subdues enemies before me'.

And David's God is our God and He wants us to know Him in this way just as David did as :

> Our Shelter of Love,
>> Our Fortress of Faith, and
>>> Our Secure Shield,

Oh! what amazing protection is this that He offers us continually. He is indeed the 'only one strong, safe and secure place' for each one of us to live in 24/7. What provision! What protection! This is not for the independent but for those of us who are aware of our weaknesses and vulnerability and will gladly accept what He is providing us with, and allow ourselves to be wrapped around by Him in His amazing love.

In Psalm 28:7-9 David says, 'You are my strength and my shield from every danger. When I fully trust in You, help is on the way…… You will be the inner strength of all Your people, the mighty Protector of all, the saving strength of all Your anointed ones. Keep protecting and cherishing Your chosen ones; in You they will never fall. Like a shepherd going before us, keep leading us forward, forever carrying us in Your arms.'

Could there be a safer place than being carried in the arms of our amazing Lord and Saviour – our Shepherd King? No wonder in the middle of these verses, in v8 David breaks out into....

'I jump for joy and burst forth with ecstatic, passionate praise! I will sing songs of what You mean to me!'

Oh Dear Jesus, I'm just so grateful that You not only want to protect me but You have provided each of Your children with full protection, with a full set of armour which never wears out so long as we keep wearing it and using it. Thank you that it is so comfortable that we never need to take it off, not even when we lie down to sleep. Thank you that the more we use each part of the armour the more effective it becomes in protecting us.

Ephesians 6:10-18.

Oh thank you that You have given me ...

the Belt of Truth.

You categorically said that You *are* - **THE TRUTH**

John 14:6 and in John 17:15-17 You say to Father, referring to Your disciples, "I ask that You guard (protect) their hearts from evil, ... Your Word is truth! So make them holy by the truth."

Oh thank you that if we willingly wear Your belt of Truth we will know Your protection from the evil one who seeks continually to distort the truth. He is so rightly called the father of lies. May we so get to know more of Your truth about :

You and all You are;

    about who You say we are;

        about who You say those we meet, day by day, are.

Thank you that You have given me …….

the Breastplate of Righteousness.

May Your righteousness, Your holiness be the covering that protects my heart from all the emotional attacks that the enemy sends in my direction. Thank you that You want to provide me with Your righteousness and I don't have to manufacture it for myself.

Thank you that you have given me……..

the Shoes of the Gospel of Peace.

Lord the shoes that You give me will fit perfectly. You know the terrain that You have called me to walk through day by day. They are not slippers to be put on just when I'm tired, nor are they hobnail boots that will crush whatever I tread on, but they are the Good News of Peace that You want me to share wherever You send me and You want me to wear them 24/7. These shoes are not for taking off when I enter someone's house or a mosque, these are for wearing wherever I go and are appropriate footwear for any and every occasion. May I keep them beautifully clean and enjoy their comfort and protection all the time, and so walk gently, with confidence, wherever You lead me.

Thank you that You have given me…….

the Shield of Faith.

May I really learn to use this shield of Faith against all the wiles of the enemy - against doubt, against discouragement, against depression, against deceptions, against distractions and dead ends.

Thank you that the shield of a Roman soldier, which was possibly what Paul had in mind when he penned the letter to the

Ephesians, was such that when held in front of the soldier it protected his whole body from head to toe; and when standing next to other soldiers their shields collectively made a complete screen; or if they lifted their shields up over their heads horizontally they would be protected from all aerial attacks. They were made of leather and soaked in water so that they would not burn when struck by flaming arrows or be penetrated.

Thank you that You will always give me the strength and determination to keep carrying this shield and never to put it down thinking I need a rest from it. It's not heavy if I learn to use it aright and don't just swing it around and hit fellow soldiers with it but stay in my place in the team.

Thank you that You have given me …..

the Helmet of Salvation.

Oh thank you Lord that You *have* saved me but You give me the helmet of Salvation to wear all the time because You *are* saving me day by day from the lies of the evil one that seek to bombard my mind but which, with the helmet of salvation firmly on my head, I have no need to entertain. Thank you that there are no missiles too heavy or strong that this helmet cannot fend them off. May I always keep it firmly in place.

Thank you that You have given me …..

the Sword of the Spirit which is the Word of God.

You have given each of us a razor-sharp two-edged sword – the living Word of God - to use in close combat with the enemy, or, as the Roman soldiers also used it, to cut out any poisoned arrow tip that penetrated their own body before the poison spread and killed them.

Oh may I really get used to rightly handling the Word of Truth and rightly applying it firstly to my own life and then, as appropriate, when seeking to fight for others' lives.

A Prayer :

Oh thank you Lord that You have provided me with this amazing suit of armour which is so wearable wherever You put me, no matter what the spiritual climate, and in which and with which You enable me to 'stand firm and fight and having done all to stand.'

Question : Do I put the whole armour of God on and keep it on 24/7 or do I just keep it by me in case of emergencies?

Oh thank you Jesus, that not only do You want to be my Protector but You also want to be my Shelter and Refuge – that safe place that I can run into at any moment and know that I am safe and secure no matter what is going on around me or what the enemy is trying to alarm or distract me with.

As David said to God in Psalm 9:9-10 'All who are oppressed may come to You as a shelter in the time of trouble, a perfect hiding place. May everyone who knows Your mercy keep putting their trust in You, for they can count on Your help no matter what. O Lord You will never, no never, neglect those who come to You.'

And in Psalm 16:1 'Keep me safe, O mighty God. I run for dear life to You, my safe place.'

And in Psalm 17:8 'Protect me from harm; …. Yes, hide me within the shelter of Your embrace, under Your outstretched wings.'

What an amazing testimony David shares in Psalm 27

v1 'The Lord is my revelation-light to guide me along the way; He's the source of my salvation to defend me every day. I fear no one!....surround and protect me.'

v3 'My heart will not be afraid even if an army rises to attack, I know that You are there for me, so I will not be shaken.'

v4 'Here's the one thing I crave from God, ... I want the privilege of living with Him every moment in His House/His Presence, ... I want to live my life so close to Him…..'

v5 'In His shelter in the day of trouble, that's where you'll find me, He hides me there in His holiness. He has smuggled me into His secret place, where I'm kept safe and secure – out of reach from all my enemies.'

What wonderful blessings are available to each one of us if we are really craving/willing/making the effort to enjoy the privilege of living in the presence of our amazing God, taking time to find 'the sweet loveliness of His face, filled with awe, delighting in His glory and grace.' v4.

May this really be the ***one thing*** that we crave 24/7 then we shall know the reality of being kept safe and secure from all our enemies.

Oh thank you Lord that not only do You want to ***protect*** me and ***shelter*** me but You also provide Yourself as a ***city of refuge*** for me. This is so comforting and reassuring that, as in the time of Joshua when the land of Canaan was being allocated to the 12 tribes of Israel, You told them to allocate 6 cities to be known as Cities of Refuge to which any one who had inadvertently committed manslaughter could run to and they would be safe there from the revenge of thirsty relatives until a proper trial was held to determine the person's guilt or innocence. Joshua 20:1-6. Should they choose to leave the safety of the City of Refuge the person no longer had any protection and could be attacked and killed by those who wanted revenge. Jesus wants to be that Refuge for each one of us all the time, but we need to run into Him and stay there and not venture out. The wonder of the situation is that not only does He invite us to live permanently in Him but, knowing that we are guilty of all manor of crimes (sins), He has already paid the death penalty in our place so that we can live in His amazing freedom if we will stay in the Refuge He has personally provided for us.

As the Psalmist says in Psalm 46:1 'God, You are such a safe and powerful place to find Refuge, You're a proven help in time of trouble…'

May this be our daily testimony!

I'm so grateful that You are ……

My DIRECTOR

Oh, how I need Your directing in my life day by day;

    conversation by conversation;

        act of kindness by act of kindness;

            challenge by challenge.

Thank you that You say in Psalm 32:8-9 "I will stay close to you, instructing and guiding you along the pathway for your life. I will advise you along the way and lead you forth with My eyes as your guide." Oh Lord, You see the whole picture, we don't, so how wonderful that You guide us by what You see and not just by what we see. And then You chide us – "so don't make it difficult, don't be stubborn when I take you where you've not been before. Don't make Me tug you and pull you along. Just come with Me."

Oh dear Lord, may I always follow Your directions willingly, gladly, wholeheartedly and completely even if I can't see how they will work out. May I have the grace of Gideon and Joshua who were willing to carry out Your seemingly crazy directives and thus won their respective battles against the Midianites and the people of Jericho.

                                        Joshua 7:7-22, Joshua 5:13 – 6:27.

May I really live out Proverbs 3:5-7.

May I really 'Trust in the Lord completely, and not rely on my own opinions.'

May I 'with all my heart rely on You to guide me, and You will lead me in every decision I make.'

May I 'Become intimate with You in whatever I do, and You will lead me wherever I go.'

May I 'not think for a moment that I know it all, for wisdom comes when I adore You with undivided devotion and avoid everything that's wrong.'

Thank You Lord for Your promise to direct us in Jeremiah 29:11-13

> "For I know the plans I have for you," says the Lord. "They are plans for good and not for disaster, to give you a future and a hope. In those days when you pray, I will listen. If you look for Me wholeheartedly, you will find Me."

Thank You for Your promise to direct us in Isaiah 30:20-21

> 'Even though the Lord may allow you to go through a season of hardship and difficulty, He Himself will be there with you. He will not hide Himself from you, for your eyes will constantly see Him as your Teacher. When you turn to the right or turn to the left, you will hear His voice behind you to guide you saying, "This is the right path follow it."'

A Prayer : Dear Jesus, may I *always* allow You to be THE Director of my life not just A director. I invite You to be the Managing Director of every department of my life as well as the Owner and the Chairman of the Board. You alone know the best way to:

> run my life;
> > to develop my life;
> > > to increase the productivity of my life.

Jesus, from the age of 13 You worked with Joseph managing the family business and must have taken it over when Joseph died, but at the age of 12 you said to Mary and Joseph when they lost You and then found You in the Temple in Jerusalem, "Didn't you know that I must be about My Father's business?"

Lord Jesus, please be about Your Father's business in my life all day and every day so that You get all the glory.

Amen.

I'm so grateful that You are …..

My INTERCESSOR

Oh thank You that Hebrews 7:25-26 says, 'So He (Jesus) is able to save fully from now throughout eternity, everyone who comes to God through Him, because He lives to *pray continually* for them. He is the High Priest Who perfectly fits our needs…'

Jesus I'm just so grateful that You don't just pray for me occasionally, that would be amazing, but You pray for me continually, you know that I need you to do that and You willingly do it, knowing exactly what to pray for me.

And in Romans 8:34 it says 'Who then is left to condemn us? Certainly not Jesus the Anointed One! For HE gave His life for us and even more than that, He has conquered death and now is risen, exalted, enthroned by God at His right hand. So how could He possibly condemn us since He is *continually praying for our triumph?*'

Oh Jesus You don't just pray for us to 'get by' but You are praying for us to TRIUMPH! May we live humbly in that expectation day by day.

Dear Jesus, thank you so much that we have a record of Your prayer both for Your disciples and for all who would come to faith in You down the ages through their witness. So that means You prayed specifically for us too and are continuing to do so, with the Holy Spirit, before the Father.

What did You pray then? And what are You praying for us now?

Let's read John chapter 17 slowly phrase by phrase.

Here are a few of the wonderful nuggets from Jesus' prayer :

Nugget 1,

v9 -11 "So with deep love, I pray for My disciples. I'm not asking on behalf of the unbelieving world but for those who belong to You, those You have given Me ……Holy Father I ask that by the power of Your name, protect each one that You have given Me, and watch over them so that they will be united as one, even as We are one."

Jesus is praying for ALL His disciples – then and now – to be as united as He and the Father are.

They had complete unity – Trinity Unity actually - and for each generation, since He first prayed this, He is still continually praying for His 'now' disciples to live in this level of unity. How willing are we for Him to see the answer to this urgent request prayed with deep love? Do we even think that it really matters if we have real unity with the other Christians in our village, town, city, country or world? This is why He asks for each one of us to be protected not that we would have a comfortable life, but that the power of Father's name would protect us from criticising one another, gossiping about one another, thinking ourselves better than other groups of His disciples.

In what practical ways does Jesus want *us* to demonstrate this wonderful unity?

Nugget 2

v13 "But now I am returning to You so Father, I pray that they will experience and enter into ***My joyous delight in You*** so that it is fulfilled in them and overflows."

Wow! Jesus is praying for us – for you and me – to experience and enter into His joyous delight in the Father to such an extent that it fills us to overflowing. Are we really willing to receive this abundance of joy that He is praying for us to experience, not just on an odd occasion, but day by day? He's not asking for us to put on a joyful mask but that His joy may be in us, and that our joy may be full. John 15:11. This is a joy that is not dependent on circumstances or other people but on our taking real time to delight in the Father with Jesus.

What a privilege!

Nugget 3

v15-16 "I am not asking that You remove them from the world, but I ask that You guard their hearts from evil, for they no longer belong to this world any more than I do."

Jesus is praying to the Father that He will 'guard our hearts from evil.'

Why does He pray this?

Surely because He knows that the enemy will do his best, or should we say, his worst, to contaminate our emotions and our thoughts as he did with Adam and Eve - 'Did God say???' satan does not want us to enjoy Nugget 2. He wants us to think that we still belong very much to this environment that he so often seems to control, but Jesus makes this amazing statement that 'we no longer belong to this world any more than He does.'

As believers do we really believe that we don't belong to this world? How much sway does this world have on our emotions, our thinking, on our actions, on our reactions?

Yes, for a while He plans for us to be 'in the world but not of it.' Are we willing to live, for the rest of our earthly life, in a 'foreign' land as an Ambassador of Heaven? Either we can contaminate our environment, in a positive way, and radiate Jesus or it can contaminate our hearts, in a very subtle way, so that we no longer bring glorious change. God wants us to be salt and light all the time, we are His ambassadors here on earth and we will only fulfil that role as we allow Him to guard our hearts day by day, moment by moment.

Nugget 4

v 17-19 "Your Word is truth! So make them holy by the truth. I have commissioned them to represent Me just as You commissioned Me to represent You. And now I dedicate Myself to them as a holy sacrifice so that they will live as fully dedicated to God and be made holy by Your truth." Jesus only spoke what He heard the Father speak and only did what He saw Him do. So he could say, with complete authority, "I am the Truth."

How careful are we to make sure that we really follow Jesus' example and spend time finding out what Father wants to say in any and every situation? How often do we assume or presume that we know what He wants us to say or do? Jesus rarely did the same thing the same way twice. When we consider that every person He has created is unique, even if identical twins, every snowflake is different and how many of those has He created since They made the world? Are we willing to get instructions for each situation from Father?

The more we know the Truth in reality, and not just in theory, the more holy we will become – as we let Father, through the Holy Spirit, open it up to us more and more.

Jesus has commissioned *us* to represent *Him* just as the Father commissioned Jesus to represent Him. Do we really see our assignment as that serious and that mind blowing? Or do we think 'Well it's OK if I just do a bit here and a bit there.'

Jesus says He dedicated Himself to *us* as a holy sacrifice so that we will live as fully dedicated to God and be made holy by Father's truth.

Is that what we signed up for? To be as fully dedicated to Father as Jesus is to us - by His dying on the cross, paying the total price for our sins, rising again and ascending to glory so that we might become citizens of heaven and be made holy by the Truth and represent Him?

Nugget 5

v20 – 23 Here is this amazing prayer from Jesus to His Father :

"And I ask not only for these disciples but also for all those who will one day believe in Me through their message. I pray for them all to be joined together as one even as You and I Father are joined together as One. I pray for them to become one *with* Us and one *in* Us so that the world will recognize that You sent Me."

He prays that all His disciples will be joined to each other as He and Father are joined together.

That's some 'joined-ness'!

He then goes on to pray specifically that not only will we be really joined unbreakably to all other disciples but that we will demonstrably be one with Himself and the Father, not to one or the other but to both. Why? So that the *world* will recognise that Father sent Jesus. Not that just a few will recognise that the Father sent Jesus, but that the whole world, through the succeeding generations, from then until He returns, will recognise Why He came.

And then it gets even more mind blowing – as He reminds Father - "for the very glory You have given to Me I have given to them"

Why? "so that they will be joined together as one and experience the same unity that we enjoy."

Do we need to ask :

'What have we done with that glory?'

Is it really evident?'

'Do we really want it?'

And then He continues in His prayer to Father– "You live fully in Me and now I live fully in them so that they will experience perfect unity, and the world will be convinced that You have sent Me, for they will see that You love each one of them with –

the same passionate love that You have for Me,"

This is staggering isn't it?

Do we live believing that Jesus lives in us and in all the other members in our church and in the church down the road?

Do we even *want* Him to live 'fully' in us or is that too radical and too demanding?

It isn't surprising that the devil does all he can to create and maintain disunity amongst Christians and churches and denominations because Jesus says that if we live in the same unity which He and the Father enjoy, and want to share with us individually and collectively, then "the world will be convinced that the Father sent Jesus and that He and He alone is the Saviour of the world."

Nugget 6

v 24 Jesus then utters another mind blowing prayer - "Father, I ask that You allow everyone that You have given to Me to be with Me where I am!"

Do we want all the Christians we know to be with us where we are, or do we prefer to only see some of them occasionally? But Jesus wants us all there **all** the time, even when we've messed up. He is so willing to forgive and draw us back close to Himself, to be with Him where He is – to be 'seated with Him in heavenly places'

Ephesians 2 : 1-9.

Why does He want us to be where He is?

His reply:"Then they will see My full glory – the very splendour You have placed upon Me because You have loved Me even before the beginning of time."

Does this sound as if He is being big-headed, proud and arrogant? I think not, those qualities are not in His character at all. He just knows how much we will enjoy seeing His glory, revelling in who

He really is, so different from our domesticated version of who He is. We will have no difficulty in dropping to our knees in adoring worship when we glimpse His astounding glory and realise that He wants to share it even with little diddy me.

Nugget 7

v25-26. The climax of Jesus' prayer for us who are His disciples – "You are My righteous Father, but the unbelieving world has never known You in the perfect way that I know You! And all those who believe in Me also know that You have sent Me! I have revealed to them who You are **and** I will continue to make You even more real to them, so that they may experience the same endless love that You have for Me, for Your love will now live in them, even as I live in them."

Jesus will continue to make Father increasingly real to us, not in theory but, by experiencing His incredible, never failing love for us as individuals as They both want, and delight, along with the Holy Spirit to live full time in us.

Are we willing for Jesus' prayer to be fulfilled in our personal lives? Do we want to have the same love-based unity that He and the Father so enjoy with Each Other with all other believers, or do we want to maintain our freedom to accuse, to criticise, to stamp our foot, to verbally punch other believers in the eye, to jump to the wrong conclusions and breed bitterness and hatred in our hearts and minds while creating a facade of Christian love for everyone?

Every time we do not love someone in the way that Jesus wants us to we are saying 'No' to His personal prayer for us. Oh! Ouch!

But every time we co-operate and desire His amazing prayer to be fulfilled we bring Him so much joy because when They live in us completely, and not just in our front room, then the world will have the opportunity to see how wonderful, amazing, all-powerful our God is.

A Prayer :

Oh! Dear Jesus, thank you SO much that You are *continually* interceding for me before the Father, and You never stop. Thank you that He always hears Your prayers and delights to answer them because You have this amazing permanent bond of love between You.

Dear Holy Spirit, please will You enable me to co-operate full-time with Jesus' prayer and not hold back in any way that would prevent Father granting His huge desire for me to live in real unity day in, day out.

May I bring You all, great joy by revelling and marinading in Your wonderful, encompassing, healing love 24/7.

Amen.

I'm so grateful that You are ....

My COMFORTER

Oh Lord, I'm so grateful that You want to be my Comforter –
> One Who comes to me with strength,
>> One Who comes along side me to fortify me,
>>> One Who understands my weaknesses and

knows what I'm in need of and how to get it.

Jesus while You were on earth, as You walked the land of Israel You *com-fort*ed the needy people You met in order to strengthen them.

In Matthew 11:28 You said, " ***Come*** unto Me – all who are heavy laden and I will give you rest," so that they would be *fort*ified, strengthened to carry Your burdens and Your yoke which You said are light and easy.

In Mark 6:31 You said to Your disciples, "***Come*** with Me by yourselves to a quiet place and get some rest." Why? To be *fort*ified for the next event.

In John 6:37 You said, "All you thirsty ones, ***come*** to Me! ***Come*** to Me and drink!" Jesus You knew that we can go many days, if necessary, without food but without fluid we very quickly become weak. But You are the LIVING WATER and You invite us to Come and drink. When we ***Come*** and drink we will be *fort*ified. Oh thank you that You are never in a drought season. Your supply of Living Water never dries up or runs out, we can always drink as much as we want whenever we want and You will fortify us.

You indeed want to COMFORT us, strengthen us, give us hope day by day, may we be willing to receive Your comfort in whatever form You want to give it to us.

In Psalm 23:4 David says to You, 'Your rod and Your staff they *comfort* me.' The rod was the tool the shepherd used to ward off predators; and the staff was the tool he used to guide the sheep.

Together they provided comfort to the sheep. If they had a good shepherd, one who knew how to use these tools well, they knew they were secure, they knew that they were safe even in the presence of their enemies, even in the valley of the shadow of death.

The shepherd would use His staff with it's hook to help the sheep stay on the path or to get them back on the path as they wandered or slipped off it. Doing this the shepherd may bring short term *dis*-comfort in order for the sheep to be really comforted – secure and safe and able to move on with Him as He leads His flock through rough terrain to get to the new pastures He has for them.

A prayer:

Oh Jesus! Thank you so much that You want to be my Good Shepherd every day of my life and as such You want to comfort me – protect and guide me through every situation. Thank you that You are willing to dis-comfort me when I choose to stray from Your perfect pathway for my life in order to bring me back into Your comfort.

Thank you that when You returned to heaven You sent the Holy Spirit to be Your personal Comforter to each one who will receive You as their Saviour. You said "I will send you another Comforter, one called alongside as your helper." John 14:16-17.

May I walk in that calm assurance that the Dear Holy Spirit, sent by the Father at Your request, will be my Comforter, my Advocate, my Strengthener, my Encourager, and my Teacher of the truth Who will remind me of all that You have taught me. John 14:26 AMP.

Oh Jesus thank you for providing me with a full-time Comforter Who will never leave me nor forsake me and will always reveal more of You to me.

I am SO grateful.

I am so Grateful that You are ……….

My Salvation / Saviour / Redeemer

You have redeemed / saved me 'out of...' and 'into...' You haven't just mercifully got me 'out of...' but You have so lovingly put me 'into...' and I am SO thankful.

* You have redeemed me out of hell – into heaven – even on earth.

* You have redeemed me from my past – into Your future for me.

* You have saved me out of the distress of the storm – into Your peace in the storm.

*You have saved me out of my sin – into Your righteousness.

* You have saved me out of my death – into Your Life.

* You have saved me out of satan's clutches – into Father's embrace.

* You have saved me out of disqualification – into qualification.

* You have saved me out of the orphanage – into Your family.

* You have saved me out of my poverty – into Your riches.

* You have saved me out of my anxiety – into Your peace.

* You have saved me out of my anger – into Your forgiveness.

* You have saved me out of my stress – into Your rest.

* You have saved me out of my distance – into Your intimacy.

* You have saved me out of my abuse – into Your use.

* You have saved me out of my sickness – into your health.

* You have saved me out of my uselessness – into Your usefulness.

* You have saved me out of my prayerlessness – into Your prayerfulness.

* You have saved me out of my carelessness – into Your carefulness.

* You have saved me out of my hatred - into Your love.

* You have saved me out of my darkness --into Your light.

When You save us 'Out of..' You always save us 'Into..'

Forgive me that so often while regretting the past I forget / ignore what You have brought me 'Into..' I'm so glad to be 'Out Of..' but haven't really entered 'Into..'

* You have saved me out of myself – into Your glorious self.

* You have saved me out of my legalism – into Your freedom.

* You have saved me out of my depression – into Your joy.

* You have saved me out of my sadness – into Your gladness.

* You have saved me out of my criticising – into Your praising.

* You have saved me out of my moaning – into Your singing.

* You have saved me out of my grumbling – into Your Thankfulness.

* You have saved me out of my controlling – into trusting You.

* You have saved me out of my manipulating – into Your controlling.

* You have saved me out of my dishonouring – into Your honouring.

* You have saved me out of my self-centredness –

                                        into You-centredness.

* You have saved me out of my despair – into Your hope.

* You have saved me out of my destructiveness – into Your creativity.

* You have saved me out of my disgruntledness – into Your

                                        satisfaction.

* You have saved me out of my barrenness – into Your fruitfulness.

* You have saved me out of my arrogance – into Your humility.

* You have saved me out of my unbelief – into Your faith.

* You have saved me out of my compromise – into Your joyful abandonment.

*You have saved me out of my shyness – into Your gentle freedom.

* You have saved me out of my lethargy – into Your activity.

* You have saved me out of my emptiness – into Your fullness.

* You have saved me out of my impatience – into Your patience.

* You have saved me out of my giving-upness – into Your perseverance.

* You have saved me out of my waiting for God – into waiting on and in God.

* You have saved me out of my hardness – into Your compassion.

* You have saved me out of my meanness – into Your generosity.

* You have saved me out of my taking – into Your lavish giving.

* You have saved me out of my boredom – into Your excitement.

* You have saved me out of my indiscipline – into Your discipleship.

* You have saved me out of my inadequacy – into Your abundance.

* You have saved me out of my lack – into Your sufficiency.

* You have saved me out of my weakness – into Your amazing strength.

*You have saved me out of my hating – into your loving forgiveness.

A Prayer :

Holy Spirit please will You show me Your honest assessment of where I am in each of these amazing works of Grace, Salvation and Redemption which Jesus has paid the ultimate price for, so that I may walk in them and enjoy them consistently?

A Question to ask yourself -

Have I asked / desired / admitted that I need to be saved out of any, many or all of these negatives?

Suggestion -

Underline each negative that you recognise as having been or still is part of your life.

Another Question to ask yourself -

Am I consistently living and enjoying any, many or each of these positives?

Suggestion –

Underline, differently, any positives that you can honestly say, by God's enabling, you are enjoying consistently.

Underline, differently, any negatives that you want God to save you out of and that you are, or want to be, willing to co-operate with Him to come out of and into the positive.

Find a Scripture verse that speaks clearly about each of these positives and maybe the negatives too.

You may want to add other negatives and positives to your list.

We cannot change ourselves. We will only be changed as we choose to believe God's Word and what He says about us. As we co-operate with the Holy Spirit as He nudges, prompts and reminds us to choose to enjoy all that Jesus has done for us personally to save us and redeem us out of, then we will enjoy the fullness of the life He offers us, not occasionally but day by day consistently.

The changes will only take place as we Adore Him *often* and as we express our Gratitude from the depths of our hearts *often*.

Rejoice! Gratitude is an attitude that negatives and sin cannot co-habit with.

~ For your thoughts ~

~ For your thoughts ~

Expectancy:

And now let's consider the third request from Jesus:

"I would like the gift of your
                         E xpectancy."

Expectancy =

Anticipation,

Outlook,

Assumption.

This gift which Jesus would love us to give Him is very different from the previous two gifts of Adoration and Gratitude. Both those gifts are very positive but Expectancy while it can be very positive can also be very negative and anywhere in-between. We can experience both at the same time, for example : I may have a very high/positive expectation of my favourite team that they will win the next match but at the same time I may have a very low/negative expectation that I have passed my exams. Only time will tell if my expectations were realised or not.

Expectancy is often based on our, or someone else's, previous experience, for example : If I have been, or someone tells me they have been, to a restaurant and had an amazing meal I will go full of expectancy that this next meal will be just as amazing.

By the time we are young teenagers many of us will have established our expectancy levels/traits – some of us will have very positive expectations about most things and are very surprised when things don't turn out the way we expect. Others of us may have very negative expectations and again are very surprised when things don't turn out as we expect. Others have more varied levels of expectation.

If through our lives we have been let down by many key people we may find it hard to *expect* God to keep His promises to us. If we have had many negative things spoken over our lives we may find it hard to *expect* God to say anything positive about us instead we are inclined to say, 'Oh God's punishing me' if something difficult or unpleasant happens. Also the longer we have to wait for something to happen we generally become more negative in our expectation. However, if the gifts of Adoration and Gratitude are already being given, by us, to Jesus, not just for His birthday, but day by day, then our levels of positive expectancy will grow and we will come more easily to 'Rejoice in the Lord always' Philippians 4:4, even in the midst of very difficult, maybe dark situations as the Apostle Paul did who gave us this exhortation.

As I sat down to write this chapter having tried to start it so many times, over many months, and got nowhere I was challenged by the last question in the devotional book I was reading one morning – 'How *expectant* are you for a miracle today?' So I chose to believe that the Holy Spirit would give me what He wanted and picked up my pen, yes, they still have their uses! - with much greater expectation, and now I have several further questions for us to ponder on and to ask the Holy Spirit to share what He considers our honest answers should be.

1) Do I *expect* God to call me to a 'higher' more intimate walk with Him and not be content with a mediocre walk (where I am now)?

2) Do I *expect* God to challenge some of my actions/ reactions if they don't bring Him joy?

3) Do I *expect* miracles to happen on a regular basis in my life? Things which I can't do but only He can?

4) Do I *expect* God to direct my path or just to bless my plans?

5) Do I *expect* and allow God to stretch me and enable me beyond my natural abilities and comfort zones?

6) Do I really live in Ephesians 3:20? When I commit the new day to Him do I really *expect* Him to 'do exceeding abundantly above all I can ask, think or imagine?' To what extent do I *expect* His power to work in me so that He gets the glory?

7) Do I really *expect* God to listen and respond to my prayers especially for my family 'prodigals' to return to Him even if I've been praying for them for years?

8) Do I really *expect* Him to speak personally to me through many different ways or do I limit Him to just one or two 'safe' ways?

9) Do I really *expect* Him to enjoy my Adoration and Gratitude or do I think He's far too busy with others?

10) Do I really *expect* Him to ask me, and expect me, to fulfil the great commission in Matthew 10:8? Or do I expect Him not to ask me because I'm too....? - that is to deny His ability to enable and that He is really THE all powerful God.

If we really spend time in Adoration for who He is, and Gratitude for all He has done, is doing, and will do, on a regular basis, then our levels of *Expectancy* will rise consistently as we fix our focus on our Almighty, Majestic, Amazingly Creative and all-loving God – Father, Son and Holy Spirit.

God wants us to be excited about what He has done, is doing and will do in our personal lives, in our families, in our neighbourhood, our village/town/city, indeed, in all parts of the world.

He IS at work but do we see it? Do we even *expect* to see Him at work?

Please **listen** to the word 'Expectancy'

when we hear it, it could be written as

'EXPECT - and - SEE'.

This is the Expectancy God would love us to have each day, that no matter what goes on in our lives we will -

'Expect and See' Him at work mightily and rejoice and Adore Him more and be increasingly Grateful which will result in our having greater Expectancy - the gifts He would love to receive from us daily.

God wants us to Expect and See much more than our Salvation/ our free ticket to heaven. It is vitally important that we are certain of our Salvation because of what Jesus did for us on the Cross – dying in our place for our sins and rising again having defeated the enemy. But He also wants us to enjoy a life full of positive Expectancy that if we walk in accordance with His will we will see miracles of all sorts, shapes and sizes on a regular basis.

When we are expectant of someone or something our attention is fixed on them – be it a devoted father coming home after an absence or a volcano threatening to erupt nearby.

As Christians we have –

a doting, devoted Father,

a delivering, dynamic Saviour, and

a demonstrative, directing Holy Spirit.

Each of Them longing to spend all of every day with us personally. That should get us out of bed each morning with delightful expectancy to face whatever is on the agenda.

Our inadequacies are Jesus' opportunities for miracles.

But above all we should be Expecting to see His glorious return and live in the light of His SOON coming.

One of the main Bible Translating Missions reckons that due to all the modern technology now available to them, every people group, will have some, if not all, of the Bible in their own language by 2033 either in print or as a solar audio Bible, we know that this must happen before Jesus returns.

No one knows the exact time or details of His return but lets focus on the reality that we don't have long to fulfil the Great Commission, and so expect and welcome the Holy Spirit to enable us each day to fulfil our exciting task.

We have *Good News of Great Joy*.

Let's **Expect** and **See** the opportunities He gives us every day to share it with those we meet, with His love and compassion.

~ For your thoughts ~

~ For your thoughts ~

~ **For your thoughts** ~

Part 2

Now let's enjoy the

    A doration

        G ratitude and

            E xpectancy

of the different characters in the original

    Christmas story.

The A doration

G ratitude

E xpectation of Zechariah.

Luke 1.

Zechariah was an old man v18 with an old wife but their lives were ones of adoration – they fervently loved from their hearts, minds, bodies, souls and spirits v6 – they were righteous in the sight of God, walking blamelessly in all the commandments of the Lord (Lord not law).

This was not legalism this was love, fervent love; fervent love in spite of their huge disappointment that they had no children, that Almighty God whom they served unreservedly had not answered their prayers but had left them socially embarrassed. Still they walked blamelessly – still they served, still Zechariah went up to Jerusalem whenever it was his turn to officiate in the Temple, still Elisabeth was prepared to stay at home and they didn't blame God, with the result that God considered them 'blameless.'

They didn't blame - so they were considered blameless.

If I blame - I am no longer blameless.

Their gift to God of Adoration and Gratitude in spite of their stigma and emptiness meant that they were ready and available to host

John the Baptist – Jesus' necessary forerunner – such a one off character with such a unique job to do.

> Their Adoration led to their availability.

Their consistent fervent love meant they were ready for God to use them anywhere, any way, any time.

Is my adoration such that I don't care / mind whether God uses me or not?

Whether He answers my prayers or not?

Whether I am socially – even within the Church – acceptable or not?

Is my offering of 'incense' a formality or a fervent delight and, therefore, a sweet smelling offering to the Lord?

The word 'fervent' has a ferocity about it. It has a tenacity about it – it's a lot more than 'keen' - it's intense.

Fervent love will carry on loving no matter what is thrown at it. This is how Jesus and Father love us and They delight when we adore Them in like manner.

Zechariah showed his Adoration by the time he spent in the Temple – yes, doing what he was called / obliged to do but doing it righteously.

We don't know about his Gratitude at this time but it must have been there as he 'walked righteously in the sight of God' and lack of Gratitude would not have been righteous but his level of Expectation must have been zero relating to their prayer for a child being answered. How many times since they were married had they petitioned God for a child? 100s if not 1000s. They got passed asking – there was no point – it was too late – it was no longer possible.

No Expectation, but their Adoration and Gratitude were still intact.

Is our Expectation high because of Who God is or because of what we want?

Zechariah's Expectation at that moment was to complete his task and go back out to the people as he had so many times before and then go home as before.

He was NOT expecting an angelical visitation – he was all on his own, he didn't have other priests with him, he didn't have Elisabeth with him and people were waiting for him outside.

This was a scary dilemma v 12; he was troubled; and fear took possession of him.

Probably all angelic visitations are unexpected and certainly many of them created an Expectancy of fear in the recipient but in v13 the angel called him by name and told him 'not to be afraid because his petitions – prayers of the years – HAD been heard' and now was the right time for the answer – not 10 years or 20 years previously but NOW.

John the Baptist had to be born at the time Jesus needed him not when Zechariah and Elisabeth wanted him. Years earlier Mary would not have been old enough to carry Jesus. The proclamation by Gabriel came with so many amazing promises v14-17 but because of his 'long stay' in a place of non-expectancy the promise did not enable Zechariah to break through to Expectation. In spite of his Adoration – fervent love of God – and Gratitude he was living in negativity regarding his / their future – they would remain childless.

BUT ....NOW!

What promises!   What encouragement!

V13-17,   Your prayers were heard.
　　　　　Your wife will have a son.
　　　　　　You will have joy and exultant delight.
　　　　　　Many will rejoice over his birth.
　　　　　　　He will be great and distinguished in the
　　　　　　　　　sight of the Lord.
　　　　　　　He will be filled with & controlled
　　　　　　　　by the Holy Spirit even in and
　　　　　　　　from his mother's womb.
　　　　　　　　　He will ……. He will ………

v18 and YET there was still huge doubt – no Expectancy
　　　' How shall I know and be sure of this?'

v19-20 Sometimes God has to act drastically to raise our level of Expectation and belief –

　　9 months of silence -

　　　no longer able to vocalise doubt -

　　　　not able to vocally share his encounter with an angel -
　　　　　　　　Gabriel at that!

　　Their expectation had been to sit on God's redundant shelf for the rest of their lives, they were still fervent in their Adoration and Gratitude but believed they had well and truly passed their 'sell by' date in God's economy.

What is my expectancy level?

Do I feel that my prayers / petitions have not been heard?

Do I feel on the shelf and redundant in kingdom matters?

Zechariah acknowledges that he and Elisabeth are not able to fulfil the word Gabriel has spoken. They are past it but that had not stopped them being faithful, persistent and constant in their Adoration and Gratitude to God. They still worshipped and adored. They still fulfilled the role they did have faithfully, blamelessly and uncomplainingly.

It was because they were totally aware of their inability to fulfil this 'Word' that it was safe for God to use them because HE would get all the glory and honour – not them.

If we think we 'can' God probably 'won't' or will delay until we recognise that we 'can't.' If our expectancy level is high in regard to what God will have us do but our adoration and gratitude levels are low we are probably heading for a fall, maybe even a big fall.

Our Expectancy must be in what HE will do with or without us. What was the effect of Zechariah's lack of Expectancy on others?

v21 - 'The people were kept waiting'

Do I keep people waiting because I don't believe and so God is hindered in His timing?

v22 - 'He was unable to speak'

He was not able to fulfil his duties in the normal manner – communication was reduced to sign language.

Does my lack of belief in what God has said reduce my ability to communicate His truth to others, to those who are waiting to hear from God via me?

But then he went home – that must have been a hilarious conversation and a night like they'd not had for many, many years – they were BOTH expecting and they weren't disappointed because the God they adored, and were so full of gratitude to, had appointed:

NOW was **THE** time!

In spite of Zechariah's silence their levels of adoration and gratitude as well as expectancy must have rocketed. What laughter, what joy, what exultant delight must have filled those 9 months.

v57 – 9 months later Elisabeth gave birth to a son!

What was the result of their A doration

G ratitude

E xpectancy ?

The neighbours and relatives heard that the Lord had shown great mercy on Elisabeth and they rejoiced with her.

Does my -

A doration

G ratitude

E xpectancy cause others to see God's mercy and rejoice with me?

But even this amazing miracle and delight didn't shift the neighbours' and relatives' expectancy, they still expected them to follow the 'tradition' and call the baby – Zechariah.

Does my -

    A doration

        G ratitude

            E xpectation cause others to allow their expectancy levels – outlook - to shift and let go of traditions?

What of Zechariah and Elisabeth's relationship to tradition? Did they decide to compromise and call the baby John Zechariah or Zechariah John? They would still have been obeying the angelic command by including the name John wouldn't they?

But their levels of

    A doration

        G ratitude

            E xpectancy were such that they were content to let go of tradition and be uncompromisingly obedient.

Individually, both Elisabeth and Zechariah categorically declared 'He shall be called John;' 'His name is John;' and that obedience opened Zechariah's mouth v64 and out poured such a torrent of praise and blessing and thanks to God that awe v65 and reverential fear came upon all their neighbours. And these things were discussed throughout the hill country of Judea, because even at 8 days old it was evident that the hand of the Lord was upon him for some very special purpose.

Just a comparatively small break with tradition in obedience to God had widespread repercussions.

How particular am I in following detailed instructions? Even if others don't think it's right?

What traditions do I hold onto which God might ask me to let go of?

Zechariah's obedience v63 brought him instant freedom of speech which exploded into levels of

    A doration

        G ratitude

            E xpectancy he had presumably never known before as he was filled with the Holy Spirit v67 and controlled by Him and prophesied.

It was like a dam breaking – 9 months of pent up verbal Adoration and Gratitude now with mega Expectancy broke out from Zechariah's whole being, this was not just from his head – it was his whole mind, body, strength, soul, and spirit. This came out of every part of him unreservedly not worrying what others were thinking.

This was from him to God but it overflowed from him to others around for miles; blessing them; encouraging them; giving them excellent news for the future in spite of all the tyranny and oppression they were living under.

v65 What effect does my A doration

        G ratitude

            E xpectancy have on other people?

Does it cause awe and reverential fear to come on all my neighbours?

Does it cause what I say to be talked about throughout the area?

Does it cause people to question 'What is happening?' 'What is God doing?' 'What is special about .....?' because they see the hand of the Lord so evidentially on a person or a place or a situation.

v64 Surely it was because of his level of

    A doration

        G ratitude

            E xpectancy

that Zechariah v67 was filled with and controlled by the Holy Spirit that his

    A doration

        G ratitude

            E xpectancy had made him completely available to God, for the Holy Spirit to fill him and use him to speak out prophetic words he had no idea about or how they would be fulfilled.

Oh that my gift of A doration

        G ratitude

            E xpectation might make me that available for the Holy Spirit to fill, control and use however He sees best.

v68 --What a transformation!

In v18 Zechariah says to the angel Gabriel, 'How shall I know and be sure of what you've said?' and now he's declaring with complete confidence that God has done 'stuff' which was actually still future!

'Blessed.... Praised and extolled and thanked be the Lord God of Israel because He has come and brought deliverance and redemption to His people... and He has raised up a horn of Salvation for us....'

Jesus was still 30 years away from starting His 3 year ministry culminating in Him being the Deliverer and Redeemer of His people.

In 9 months Zechariah's Adoration, Gratitude and especially Expectancy had grown exponentially, had shifted to a completely new level. 9 months of silence, 9 months of watching a bump grow, 9 months of pondering, 9 months of laughter.

What God can do with someone who is available for 9 months. When Expectancy is added to Adoration and Gratitude there is a seismic shift.

Yes, they had the benefit after a while of seeing the 'bump' grow. There is no guarantee and there will be a visible 'bump' before God births whatever He has promised. He may require a greater level of faith / expectancy as we are living the other side of the Cross and Resurrection and Pentecost.

They were not just excited / expectant for themselves. They were excited and expectant for the whole nation. 'He has come and brought deliverance and redemption to His people' - the whole of Israel v69-75. The Old Testament prophecies, which he knew by heart, have suddenly become alive and relevant. Zechariah believes they are for NOW, not some vague time in the all too distant future – they are for now. He sees them as already happened although they haven't, such is the level of his expectancy – this is not false expectancy, this is real, genuine Holy Spirit fanned expectancy which has filled their whole beings to bursting point because of the enormous increase in their Adoration and Gratitude.

What did he become SO sure of? v71-74 'Deliverance from our enemies and from the hand of all who detest and pursue us with hatred and from the hand of our foes.'

For what purpose was this deliverance to come? 'To make true and show the mercy and compassion and kindness promised by God in His covenant to bless and that we might serve Him fearlessly in holiness, divine consecration and righteousness within His presence all the days of our lives.' This was not just making things nice, pleasant, easy, or enjoyable. Sometimes it was, but sometimes it was not. But salvation and deliverance give the option / opportunity to enjoy the mercy, compassion and kindness God had promised and enables us to serve Him fearlessly - without fear – yes! without fear in holiness and righteousness. Fearlessly but with humility not arrogance; with divine consecration and righteousness not just sometimes but in His presence ALL the days of our lives – this is His deliverance - if we will accept it and walk in it. It's permanent, it's from now for the rest of our lives, it's not occasional. This was not temporary good news, this was / is complete, on-going for the rest of our lives if we choose to live 'in accordance with the everlasting principles of righteousness within His presence all the days of our lives.'

There is nothing that our Redeemer cannot deliver us from.

Now full of A doration

    G ratitude and

        E xpectancy Zechariah can not only take on board that the Deliverer, Redeemer, Holy One of Israel is at last coming but also the words spoken to him by Gabriel v14-17 about this little 8 day old in his arms v76, 'But you, little one, shall be called the prophet of the Most High, you shall go before the face of the Lord to make ready His ways'. He understood that John was literally to prepare the way for Jesus to come.

Jesus still needs 'Way Preparers.' Those who, in any situation where they are placed, will prepare the way for Him to come, to land and bring transformation. They cannot bring it, they can only, but essentially, prepare the place – remove the boulders, those things which stand in the way. They bring and give through their own experience of the knowledge of salvation, through the forgiveness and remission of their sins, by introducing people to the tender-hearted mercy and loving kindness of our God. They make way for the Light to shine in the darkness and in the shadow of death. They guide and direct people into the way of peace.

Zechariah and Elisabeth prepared the way for John through their

> A doration
> G ratitude
> E xpectancy

and John in turn prepared the way for Jesus through giving himself entirely to the calling on his life v76 'to go before the face of the Lord to make ready His ways.'

This is the supreme calling of every Child of God. This is a 24/7 calling which the Holy Spirit wants to grow us into just as He did Zechariah and Elisabeth and then John – are we willing for the cost of this?

To be continually giving Jesus my gift of A doration
> G ratitude
> E xpectancy

every day of the year not just at Christmas?

As A doration

    G ratitude

        E xpectancy pour out of us so we will be preparing the way of the Lord, for Him to save / transform people, areas, nations.

There is no negativity in A doration

    G ratitude or

        E xpectancy because our gaze is focused on the One who is completely worthy, and not on all we may see around us. The longer we really focus on Him the greater will be our expectation and the boulders will diminish, melt, or get up and run away and Jesus will be able to do what He came to do – to carry out His Holy Covenant to bless, to bring and give the knowledge of salvation to His people.

Am I willing to do this for 9 months and see what freedom this gives God to work in my family?..... in my Church? ...... in my area?......in my work place?

What does the gift of A doration

    G ratitude and

        E xpectancy look like in real practical
                terms for me?

The A doration
G ratitude
E xpectation of Elisabeth.

Luke 1.

Married to a priest but also in her own right a descendent of Aaron – the very first High Priest. Elisabeth and Zechariah would both have been steeped in the Old Testament, the Word of God. Had she not been barren she would have been very highly regarded, but being childless was a serious failure in the prevailing culture. Was that why, we are told in v39, she and her husband lived in a village in the hill country of Judea and not in a town or city nearer to Jerusalem where Zechariah had to go regularly to serve in the Temple?

How much antagonism must they, but she in particular, have suffered since their marriage? After all it would be considered the woman's fault that they had no child. But in spite of years of unanswered prayers v6 tells us that 'They were both lovers of God, living virtuously and following the commandments of the Lord *fully.*' Following the commandments of the Lord fully would have meant that she was 'loving the Lord her God with every passion of her heart, with all the energy of her being, and with every thought that was within her and loving her friend/neighbour as she loved herself,' just as Jesus summarized the 10 commandments in Matthew 22:38-39.

She was obviously not blaming God for years of unanswered prayer, and no matter what the stigma of being childless, or how much it hurt, she was ministering to those around her, and she was counted 'blameless.' What a beautiful assessment of her character and her relationship with God.

How often do we/do I blame God for apparently unanswered prayers? How often does my resentment about unanswered prayers hinder God using me to minister to friends, family and neighbours?

Imagine her surprise, she'd got everything ready for Zechariah's return from his stint of duty in the Temple in Jerusalem. He would have been weary from the long walk but she would have been so eager to hear all the news/gossip that he had gleaned while there, she would have wanted to hear what duties he had been allotted and how it had all gone and all she got was – **silence**! How do you convey without words that you've had an angelic visitation and not just from any old angel but from Gabriel himself, and that the message he had received was just mind-boggling and literally out of this world?

Oh the patience Elisabeth must have had to exercise as she waited for Zechariah to write on a tablet what had happened, all the little details she would have longed to hear but so much more difficult when the sharer is dumb and you don't use sign language or have any modern technology. She must have wondered if her husband of so many years had lost his mind, be suffering from dementia or whatever else? But she took him at his word and a couple of months later knew that what he had told her was true. Now they were 'expecting' and expectant.

How they must have laughed and laughed, time and time again at the bizarre situation they found themselves in – it had to be God! They had tried and tried for years to conceive, and they had prayed and prayed for years for God to give them a child all to no avail and NOW – in their old age - God answers and gives them the most amazing message as to who their son would be, what he would do, and what his name was to be.

They were a couple that God could trust because they had really learnt over the years to trust Him.

How much do we /do I really trust God with day to day living and insurmountable problems? Or do we think that we have to sort /solve them ourself?

Elisabeth had been willing, for so many years, to let Zechariah leave her at home in the village in the hills while he went and performed his required duties. That must have been so hard.

But she was 'blameless' in her response, and now she had the most amazing promises about this baby she was carrying – v15

'He will be filled with the Holy Spirit while still in her womb.' Wow! What would that be like she must have wondered. v17 'He was to go before the Lord as a forerunner, with the same anointing as Elijah the prophet.' Wow! Again! - Elijah – their great prophet? But she was also told v14 'that her baby would bring them much joy and gladness.'

Her level of Gratitude must have sky-rocketed that God had seen fit to use them in such a special way after all these years of painful waiting and expecting nothing. Now she was truly full of Expectancy, and enjoying God giving her the necessary daily strength to carry the babe full term even in her old age.

Is it any surprise that Mary, soon after her encounter with the angel Gabriel, goes to visit Elisabeth having been told by her angelic visitor that her elderly aunt was now 6 months pregnant? If anyone was going to understand Mary's predicament caused by divine intervention, surely it would be her. What a huge encourager Elisabeth must have been to this young pregnant teenager as she walked 6 months ahead of her through her own pregnancy. Even if there had been pre-natal classes in Nazareth it would not have been great for Mary to go to them. She would have been mocked, ridiculed at best - stoned at worst. But she could 'escape' to Elisabeth's and have loving, one to one pre-natal care on a daily basis from someone with very up-to-date experience. And no doubt Joseph would have been glad that she was in a 'safe' place, where she would be understood.

But not only did Elisabeth pour out Adoration and Gratitude as their Expectancy increased but she had the capacity to adore and be thankful to God for what he was doing for Mary. As her niece entered the house she was filled to overflowing with the Holy Spirit and worshipped and the babe within her 'danced with ecstatic joy.'

If God is growing/birthing something in us do we take the time and energy to worship and adore our amazing God for what He is birthing in others? Are we filled with gratitude for what He is doing in them even if it seems more important than what He is birthing in us? Or are we so blinkered that we are only centred on our own 'Baby?'

If we are '6 months pregnant' with something God is growing in us, do we make the time and effort to encourage and help those who are just beginning their 'pregnancy?' Do we provide a 'safe place' for them to develop their 'soon to be born baby?'

In Hebrew culture at that time a newly expectant mother would do nothing for the first 3 months but rest, so Mary was not going to be any help to Elisabeth as she found it harder and harder to waddle around, to pick things up, to carry the shopping, to clean the house or do the cooking, and she was another mouth to feed but none of that soured their relationship. They were both full of increasing Adoration, Gratitude and Expectancy!

Did Elisabeth and Zechariah talk/sign about Abraham and Sarah who had a similar experience of having their firstborn in their very old age, Genesis 21:1–22:19 and wondered how they had been chosen by God to be in a very similar position? What worship, adoration, wonderment must have flowed daily out of their beings.

The 9 months was up and Elisabeth gave birth to a healthy baby boy – they hadn't needed a test to find out it's sex, because God had told Zechariah to name the baby 'John' – but the rejoicing friends and neighbours didn't believe Elisabeth when she told them that the baby's name was John and had to revert to asking the father even though they had got used to listening to Elisabeth for the last 9 months. Emphatically he wrote 'His name is John' and at that point his speech returned and he praised God, filled to overflowing, with the Holy Spirit. Wow! What a relief for Elisabeth that after 9 months of silence her husband could now talk without any problem.

Together they could Adore their amazing, miracle working God, with hearts full of Gratitude living daily in Expectation of how God would fulfil the prophecies concerning their so special son whose birth was to 'bring them much joy and gladness.'

A Prayer :

Oh dear Holy Trinity, thank you that we are never too old or too young for you to birth new things in us or through us. May we, like Elisabeth, co-operate with You and Adore You for who You are as well as what You are doing. May we, by Your enabling, dear Holy Spirit, carry 'it' to full term and not abort or miscarry what you are growing in us.

May we also rejoice in what You are growing in others and really encourage them in their 'pregnancy' and as they nurture their new-born too.

Thank you that You will supply all our needs as we continue to Adore You with much Gratitude and Expectancy in our hearts.

Amen.

The A doration
G ratitude and
E xpectancy of
Mary and Joseph

Part 1

Mary's expectations must have been on a non-stop roller-coaster. Happily engaged to a 'righteous man full of integrity' who was a true descendant of David, - how prestigious was that? And he already had a steady job as a carpenter so his work would always be in demand meaning there would always be a regular income and secure future to look forward to and in which to bring up children. They wouldn't be rich but they would have sufficient.

Mary had a year to prepare for her marriage – what a joy, what delightful expectations were hers.

When   SUDDENLY!

Literally – 'Out of the blue'

an angel appeared in front of her,

and not just any old angel but the angel Gabriel who told her 'The Lord is with you and so you are anointed with great favour.'

Seeing her expectancy level plummet through the floor he said, 'Do not yield to your fears Mary, for the Lord has found delight in you and has chosen to surprise you with a wonderful gift .....' and concluded by assuring her that 'Not one promise from God is empty of power, for NOTHING is impossible with God!'

And her response? 'As His servant, I accept whatever He has for me. May everything you have told me come to pass.'

And the angel - left her!

Left her - to tell Joseph, her fiance, that she would be pregnant but not with his child – an offence punishable by stoning.

Left her - to tell her parents – what a disgrace! – pregnant out of wedlock.

Left her - with about a 90 mile walk to visit her very elderly, very pregnant relative Elisabeth who lived up in the hill country of Judea with her husband Zechariah who had also had a mind-boggling visit from the angel Gabriel 6 months previously.

What a huge mixture of emotions/expectations must have flooded her mind and heart as she weighed the pros and cons of Gabriel's message.

Wonderful to be favoured by God -

                Horrific to be ostracised by your family.

Amazing to be someone God wants to use –

                But ghastly to contemplate the cost.

But the angel had said, 'Don't yield to your fears.'

What about us? - You and Me? - Are we really willing for God to 'birth' something through us – something which we cannot bring about ourselves? Are we walking daily in Adoration and Gratitude as Mary obviously was when she burst into song when she arrived at Elisabeth's? 'My soul is ecstatic, overflowing with praise to God! My spirit bursts with joy over my life-giving God …….!'

This Adoration/worship didn't just happen at this isolated moment, this must have become her way of life as she grew through her childhood and into her teens, loving to use the Psalms in praise to God. Not only was she precious to God - as we all are - but He was so precious to her.

Can we really say with Mary, 'As His servant, I accept whatever He has for me' without adding any 'yes buts…' or 'if onlys…'

She had no idea what it would cost her, but she was still there 33 years later at the foot of that horrific cross.

And what of Joseph's expectations? So excited that Mary, the most God-fearing, beautiful girl in the village had agreed to become his wife. The most idyllic match-made in heaven? He'd begun getting the house ready for her arrival in a year's time as only a carpenter could – all the thoughtful touches that would improve his bachelor pad and turn it into a delightful home for the two of them and later with children as well. Yes, his expectations of the near future were running pretty high

When….. SUDDENLY!

He was shocked beyond belief by Mary's news – was it true anyhow or just an excuse? - This supposedly God-loving girl pregnant and claiming it wasn't by a man?

His expectations of a happily married family life with Mary had just crashed out of the window. Whatever was he to do? He knew what others would do but he loved her – what *was* he to do? Was he really to stone her? No he couldn't, he loved her too much. He would try and divorce her quietly, discreetly.

'Oh why had he bothered to put those new shelves up? Why had he spent so much time lovingly making a beautiful double bed?

Why? Why? Why?

His expectations were way below zero both for his own future and for Mary's.

He was so exhausted in every way trying to work out what to do and how to cope with his shattered emotions and expectations that he fell asleep and as he slept he had a supernatural dream - an angel appeared to him in clear light, called him and Mary by name – so no mistaking the message was for him - confirming that Mary's explanation of her pregnancy was true, and who the baby would be and what His name was to be, and that he, Joseph was to marry her.

Wow! That was some wake-up from his dream! What a rollercoaster of expectations. Now he could finish getting the house ready. Now he could marry her after all, - what a delight! amazing ! But what about all the local negative gossip not only about Mary but about him as well. - How ostracised would they be? How could he protect her from it all? This would be anything but a delight. And what about who this baby was to be and the huge responsibility of looking after him and providing for him? Expectations coloured with fear, feelings of inadequacy, confusion but still he did all that the angel of the Lord instructed him to do.

His expectation now? -

If he obeyed - God would work it out somehow.

And then ….. just as they were getting used to the snide remarks and the accusing looks …..GOD did another

SUDDENLY!

By causing Caesar Augustus to order the first census to be taken throughout his empire so that everyone had to travel to their home town to register, there was no opt out clause for very pregnant women, there was no postal registration, it was a compulsory journey of about 90 miles – about 5 days by donkey, if they had one, with others passing them at a much faster speed, unimpeded by the slowness of pregnancy or the slowness of a donkey. Four or five nights under the open skies. Was this God's way for them to avoid the animosity for a few days? Sadly not – all the relations from Nazareth were going to Bethlehem too. Many would have overtaken Mary and Joseph and shared the scandalous news on arrival and taken advantage of relatives spare accommodation before they could get there. The more people who overtook them the lower their expectation became of finding a 'good' place to stay. But surely an aunt, uncle or cousin would make room for them - but no! When they did get there all doors were shut – no room in the Inn but no room either in a relative's home.

Poor Joseph trying to make the journey as easy and gentle as possible for Mary, and Mary coping as best she could, either perched precariously on a donkey or walking each step of the way. What a strain on both of them! Was Mary still singing in her heart, if not out loud, the worship song she'd sung when she'd arrived at Elisabeth's 9 months earlier after a journey of a similar length? Or had her Adoration level dropped somewhat during the last 6 months, though her gratitude level must have risen when the angel had explained the situation to Joseph and he had obeyed the instructions and not divorced her but had continued to love and care for her so diligently.

But NOW, there must be somewhere, *somewhere* that she could give birth. What desperation for both of them – only the unborn baby was content. His heavenly Father had it all under control. At last they were offered the cave-like space under a house where stuff was stored and sick or frail animals were housed while the owners lived upstairs. What a relief to be offered somewhere – anywhere!

'And she brought forth her first born Son and laid Him in a manger...'

Let's sit and rest awhile with Mary and Joseph and Baby Jesus in the cave-stable.

Oh, the peace and quiet after the noise of the milling crowds outside and the agony of the birth pangs, and here in front of them, in the animal's feeding trough, was this mind-blowing miracle baby who had no human father – would anyone believe them?

As Mary leaned her tired, so tired, head on Joseph's strong, but so exhausted, shoulder they watched with awe and wonder. What was Jesus, yes they had been told by the angels to call Him Jesus, going to do? Who was He really going to be? As they mulled over the prophetic words Gabriel and the other angel had given them did they also call to mind the words of Isaiah 7:14? 'Behold a virgin shall conceive and bear a son?'

And then their peaceful pondering was gently disturbed, even though it was in the middle of the night. The ill-fitting door was quietly pushed open and in the dim light several eager, wide-eyed, weatherworn faces appeared looking so intently to see if what they were searching for was actually here.

And He was - lying in a feeding trough and wrapped in linen strips of cloth – a tiny baby just as the angel had told them and the heavenly hallelujah chorus had endorsed.

Were they excited???

From having no expectation except more of the 'same old, same old' when they started their night shift looking after the sheep on the hill outside Bethlehem they were now brimming over with expectation as they told Mary and Joseph of their angelic experience and the message that had been given to them – 'Don't be afraid, (they had been terrified) for I have come to bring you good news, the most joyful news the world has ever heard! And it is for everyone, everywhere! For today in Bethlehem a Rescuer was born for you. He is the Lord Yahweh, the Messiah ....'

Their wonder, their worship, their adoration knew no bounds. God had revealed Himself to them – the lowest of the low. And they didn't keep quiet about it! Everyone who heard their story, even in the middle of the night, was astonished and the shepherds returned to their flock ecstatic over what had happened. They praised God and glorified Him for all they had heard and seen for themselves just as the angel had said.

And Mary? ... she treasured all these things in her heart and pondered what they meant, and with that they fell asleep for a very short night.

Had the news the shepherds shared with all who would listen changed peoples attitude a bit towards Mary and Joseph? Plus the curiosity of wanting to see the baby?

Forty days later Mary and Joseph needed to go up to the Temple in Jerusalem to offer a sacrifice so no point in going back to Nazareth before then, as the journey from Bethlehem could be done in a day but several days from Nazareth. Had they been able to bring money with them to rent a house or had Joseph been able to pick up sufficient carpentering jobs after the many visitors had left the town? We don't know but by the time the Wise Men visited them they were living in a house. Matthew 2:11

But what of the impending journey to Jerusalem, to the Temple? Was this the first time they'd been as a couple? Certainly the first time they'd been as a family.

What were their levels of Adoration, Gratitude and Expectation?

Their Adoration of this amazing God who had choreographed the last 10 months of their lives in such extraordinary ways must have been fairly high!

Their Gratitude that He had brought them safely through all the really tough times and situations and that the baby had been safely delivered with no midwife or sterile environment and that Mother and baby, and Joseph, were doing well was cause for much thankfulness.

And their Expectations – that this would be a much easier and happier journey than the one from Nazareth - it wouldn't be so crowded. Special though it was to go and offer the required sacrifice for Mary's purification, it would be just the same as it would be for any new mother and baby.

And so they prepared to go.

Part 2. Luke 2.

Forty days after Jesus was born they went on their first family journey to offer the required sacrifices at the Temple – a pair of doves or pigeons as they were too poor to offer a lamb – for Mary's purification and to dedicate Jesus to God as it was required that every firstborn male should be set apart for God. Little did they realise that poor though they were they were so rich because they had a lamb with them – Yes, '*The* Lamb of God who takes away the sin of the world.'

And so they arrived at the Temple just wanting to do what was required of them in a humble and correct manner and

THERE - just THERE

was an old man standing right in front of them obviously very excited and full of Expectation, Adoration and Gratitude.

The Holy Spirit had organised this meeting. It was no coincidence that Simeon, an old man, a good man, a lover of God who kept himself pure and was eagerly looking for the imminent appearing of the 'Refreshing of Israel' was there. The Holy Spirit had revealed to him that he would not die before he met Him, and the same Holy Spirit had now prompted him to be there just as the little inconspicuous family entered the Temple.

Can the same be said about you and me? That we are really lovers of God who keep ourselves pure and are eagerly looking now for the 2nd coming of Jesus in all His glory and splendour?

Are we available for the Holy Spirit to prompt us to be in, or go to, the right place at the right time so that He can use us there for whatever purpose He chooses or are we only available when it's convenient? How receptive are our minds and hearts to see people and situations from God's perspective and not as they just naturally appear?

And, while he prophesied about who Jesus was and what He would do and also what would happen to Mary, Anna a very, very old widow, about 106 years old, who served God day and night with prayer and fasting in the Temple, came up to them and burst into a great song of praise to God for the child who Simeon had taken in his arms. From then on she told anyone who would listen to her that the anticipated Messiah had come.

And Mary and Joseph? They completed all they had come for and went back to Bethlehem pondering all that had been said and no doubt wondering what would happen next. How would these prophetic words pan out?

What was their E xpectation like now?

And their A doration?

And their G ratitude?

Are we/ am I more like Simeon and Anna – the longer they had to wait the higher their level of expectation to see God move rose. Or are we like the majority of folk – the longer we have to wait the lower our level of expectation, and gradually, imperceptibly, it turns to negative expectation? Which in turn leads to 'Oh God's forgotten me!' or 'I don't matter?'

Waiting often tests the reality of our expectation and our belief in what God has promised or in the God who has promised.

And so they went back to their little home in Bethlehem.

Part 3.

Wow! So much unexpected had happened in the last 24 hours. So much to talk about, so much to ponder, to consider quietly, soberly and deeply.

How much do we – you and I – ponder over the things God has said to us through the Bible, through other people, through dreams and visions, through angels, direct into our hearts and minds? There are more than 10 ways recorded in the Bible that God spoke to people. Do we expect to hear from Him personally? And if we do and He does speak do we take care to write down exactly what He said and then ponder it again and again until it happens or He says "Now is the time." Or do we just shrug our shoulders and say 'Well if it happens, it happens?'

Mary knew, even as a teenager, how incredibly important it was to listen to what God said and ponder and ponder it until it came to pass, even if it meant waiting for at least 33 years for some of those words spoken by Simeon to come to fruition.

Now life returned to some sort of normality – Joseph carpentering and Mary keeping house and looking after baby Jesus who was gradually growing into a delightful toddler.

'Who is this child really?' 'What will He become?' they often pondered.

The neighbours had got used to them, the visit of the shepherds had fallen into the back of their minds and they hadn't witnessed what had happened in the Temple so Bethlehem was relatively peaceful even if it wasn't sure if it was a small town or a large village but it was proud to be known as 'The city of David.' So the months went by – how many we don't know but probably more than a year since Jesus was born - when yes!

SUDDENLY!

Yet again!

Bethlehem was invaded. This time by a huge entourage of very excited foreigners. You didn't travel long distances in those days without your own team of bodyguards, your own catering/hospitality team so you could stop, rest and be provided for anywhere along your journey even in the middle of a desert or a hostile environment if need be. It was like a fully staffed and equipped 5-star hotel on legs – camel legs!

Why were they so excited? A star had reappeared – not any old star but the one they had been following for weeks, months, for probably more than a year. Had they been travelling by night to see the star more clearly? And now it had stopped over a wee rented house – not over the houses of the well-to-do or the influential – and every eye in Bethlehem was straining to see all they could of such a grandiose spectacle and so curious to know why they had come and were so excited. Did they also see the star stop over Mary and Joseph's house or was it only visible to those who were following it and were determined to find and worship the new born King of the Jews?

Had the Bethlehemites got so used to hearing Bethlehem mentioned in the Old Testament, as it was read every sabbath in the synagogue, that they had no curiosity as to what the prophesies meant or if they would happen in their lifetime? Their level of expectation regarding these prophesies appear to be non-existent, unlike that of the travellers who were brimming over with expectancy and were ecstatic beyond measure.

Were Mary and Joseph, like everyone else in Bethlehem, peering out of their windows and doors to catch a glimpse of what was happening? Why were these exquisitely dressed travellers dismounting right outside their home? Why were boxes being offloaded from one of the pack animals?

Was it Joseph who had opened the door to see out while Mary made sure that toddler Jesus didn't run out and get lost or crushed among all the people and animals?

Well the door was open and the travellers seemed to invite themselves in and as soon as they saw the young child with Mary they were overcome and, forgetting all their dignity, they fell to the floor at His feet and worshipped Him.

This was no 'token' worship, this wasn't a nod of the head or a bow, this was flat out Adoration – literally flat out, they could go no lower and these highly intelligent, very educated, wealthy men were willing to be seen like this by some of their own servants who were following them with 'the gifts.' This was authentic, real, unconcealed worship. This is what they had given up months, maybe more than a year for, and spent much money and energy to travel this far, through all sorts of terrain and weather, all to lie prostrate at the feet of a little toddler.

And how does our – yours and my – worship compare with theirs? And we don't just have a wee toddler to worship, we know He became the crucified, risen and glorified Saviour of all who would put Him first in their lives, as these Wise Men did.

Let us be wise and follow their example – wise men and women and children still seek Jesus and He will always be found by those who really seek Him and those who will worship Him no matter what others think or no matter the cost. He will never disappoint.

When eventually they got a little less horizontal they presented their gifts to Jesus.

Whatever was going through their minds as they looked around the poor rented home? Were they wondering if they'd made a big mistake and that what they'd brought was unsuitable for a toddler? Yes, they could see that the 'Gold' would come in very handy, maybe the parents could upgrade to a much better house or a palace and employ some servants to help take care of the needs of the young King of the Jews but what of the 'Frankincense' and the 'Myrrh'? They seemed so 'out of place' but like old Simeon's prophetic word they too were prophetic of the future, of Jesus' death and burial. They certainly didn't give these gifts to curry any favour, and they worshipped before giving gifts and gave out of full hearts not out of necessity.

Was there any conversation between Mary and Joseph and these amazing visitors? Did they have any language in common? It may have only been a language of Adoration of the Christ child but that would have been sufficient.

And then as SUDDENLY as they came they left and went home a different way because of a God-given dream not to go back to Herod as his desire to worship was completely phoney.

How genuine is our – yours and my – Adoration?

Worship is far more than singing hymns and songs gustily or even quietly. Does it really cost us? Is it really from our hearts or do we just enjoy singing? Adoration may well even be silent as we are overcome with awe.

Mary and Joseph must have just sat down and gasped and looked at each other and little Jesus with wide-eyed amazement. Yes! It had really happened - the gifts were still on the floor to prove it.

And the whole neighbourhood must have been agog with curiosity and gossip – first the shepherds, the lowest of the low, and now this amazingly wealthy foreign entourage – what was it all about? Who were Mary and Joseph and the little one really?

And then, no sooner had Joseph fallen asleep than he has another dream – an angel telling him to get up NOW and take Mary and Jesus and flee to Egypt as Herod was on the warpath with every intention of killing the Child even though the Wise Men had not gone back to tell him where Jesus was.

So that very night, while the Wise Men travel East in response to a God-given dream, Joseph, Mary and Jesus travel South West in response to a different God-given dream. Oh how easy for Joseph to have turned over and said, 'We'll go tomorrow,' but no! The instruction was 'Go Now' so he put together what they could carry of their possessions, including the new gifts. This was going to be a much longer journey than Nazareth to Bethlehem but thankfully Mary was no longer pregnant – and in the dead of night they crept out of Bethlehem on their way to becoming asylum seekers in Egypt.

What a shock for the neighbours next morning to find the house empty and no Mary or Joseph to fill them in on all that had happened the day before with the spectacular visitors.

It must have been some journey as they walked and walked and kept a lively toddler going in the right direction, or carried Him when He was too tired, and now they had yet another major happening to process and ponder – what was that amazing visitation all about? What were these unusual gifts about? What would they find in Egypt? How long would they need to be there?

All God had said was, 'Go Now to Egypt.' He hadn't given them all the future details but their Adoration and Gratitude must have still been growing as they pondered the last year and all that God had brought them through. And what of their Expectancy level? They had witnessed God do so many UNexpected things on their behalf that they were able to obey without hesitation because they had proved Him to be so Trustworthy. They Expected Him to be completely trustworthy, surely they lived by Proverbs 3:5-6 day by day and that enabled them to Adore Him and really be full of Gratitude.

> Obedience will lead to **greater** Expectancy
> which will lead to **greater** Gratitude
> and in turn will lead to **greater** Adoration.

God indeed had the gifts of their

A doration,

G ratitude, and

E xpectancy.

Where are we – you and I – on this journey? He is the same amazing God, and He loves us individually just as much as He did Mary and Joseph. So the choice is ours – yours and mine – day by day to be obediently available to do all He asks of us so that He can birth whatever He wants to in and through us.

Will we really   Listen,

                    Trust, and

                              Obey?

and give Him our

          A doration,

                G ratitude, and

                        E xpectancy?

The **A** doration
G ratitude
E xpectancy of the Shepherds.

Luke 2:8-18.

Shepherds – the lowest of the low in that culture. They lived out in the fields, they did not live in the town but out under the open sky keeping watch over other people's sheep. They were nobodies with probably little education, not even in the synagogue – could they even read or write? Who knows? Had they ever heard any of the Messianic prophecies? Quite possibly not. But they knew about shepherding, they knew about sheep, did they know, had they heard the 23rd Psalm? If so did they wonder who King David had been talking about when he wrote it?

'The LORD is my Shepherd.' They knew about the importance of 'green pastures and still waters' about taking sheep through difficult ravines, about dealing with the enemies – poisonous weeds in the grass, bears, lions, and other predators but did they know about the Lord being *their* Shepherd? Probably not though living out in the hills may have made them very aware of the amazing Creator as they lived through the changing seasons, as they watched the changing skies day and night.

But life for them did not do Expectancy except to expect more of the same, and that didn't lead to Adoration or Gratitude. If it did anything it led to struggle and a sense of hopelessness that things will never change, that they are going nowhere fast.

It was definitely a NON-expectant night.
Same food, same routines, same responsibilities

When SUDDENLY!

Suddenly an angel stood by them – the glory of the Lord flashed and shone all around them and they were terrified.

From no expectation they were suddenly catapulted into a terrifying expectation. Something completely unknown was happening.

Was it good or bad? Would they live or die?

v10. 'Don't be afraid' - at least the angel acknowledged where the shepherds were at. They didn't have to try and hide their fear.

But he is bringing them Good News.

GOOD NEWS!

GOOD NEWS?

Good News would lead to positive expectation not negative. Though for those whose expectations have been negative for a long time it can be very hard to change from one to the other. It can be so hard to let go of the negative.

Am I willing to let go of my negative expectations and take on board the *Good* News that God is speaking to me by one means or another?

It may be through an angel;

    or through the Word;

        or through a friend;

            or through a dream;

                or through a vision;

                    or through a thought;

                        or through a ………..

Am I willing to let go of the negative expectancy which has become an integral part of my being?

Yes I may need some help but am I willing? Willing to acknowledge it and willing to let go of it and exchange it for the

'Good News of Great Joy?'

The Good News of Great Joy is always on tap – it never runs out no matter where we are because the Great Joy is still the same yesterday, today and forever. As the angel said, it will come to ALL people and it has come to ALL people. Here we are 2000 plus years later and we have heard, read, received this same Good News which is Great Joy to those who really believe and receive it.

What difference has the angel's message to the shepherds really made in our lives?

Do we live with this Good News at the forefront of our minds day by day? Or is it 'Yes, I believe it but only think about it at Christmas or Easter or on a few other occasions, or do I only really think about it at Church or in a house group?' Or is it so real to me that the Saviour was born in Bethlehem as the Old Testament prophets said He would be, and that

He *is* The Messiah;

He *is* The Lord;

He *is* The Saviour

for ALL people, not just then, but right down the ages because He came to live as a man, (even though he was and is Almighty God) and die our death (and rose from the dead to prove it) and ascended back to heaven where He ever lives to intercede for us – to stand in the gap for us – so that we can be lovingly accepted by our Heavenly Father whose judgement and justice has to be satisfied as well as His mercy?

So as He looks at His beautiful, amazing but crucified, blood-stained Son He says to Jesus, 'Yes, if you died for this one, he or she are welcomed in My Kingdom so long as they have accepted what You did for them, if they have accepted the covering and the cleansing of Your shed blood.'

How amazing is that shed blood of Jesus! It has never run out, and it will never run dry. Jesus is continually pouring out His precious blood so that anyone at anytime in history who believes in Him and what He has done by dying and rising again can say, 'He did it even for me, a sinner so guilty – that's why I love Him now that I understand He suffered so much by dying and He did it for me.'

Anyone who can really say that will be welcomed and received not as a grovelling sinner – which we are – but as a much loved son or daughter of the King of Kings because we can say in reality and not just in theory :

Jesus is *my* Messiah;

Jesus is *my* Lord;

Jesus is *my* Saviour;

and that will cause us to live lives full of A doration,

G ratitude and

E expectancy

because our NOW and our future are completely safe in His hands whatever our situations look like.

The angel gave the Shepherds the Good News – the theory – but they had to ACT upon the information in order for the Good News to become Great Joy.

Are we *acting* on all the theory we've read, been taught or learned about Jesus? Or is it still just theory?

Or did it years ago become a living reality and my life had a measure of A doration

G ratitude and

E xpectancy but everyday life has dulled my heart and mind?

In John 10:10 Jesus said, "I am come that they might have life and have it more abundantly," not just in theory or just in the future but NOW.

He invites each of us to move from theory to reality, from hearing a message to living the message – the shepherds 'went with haste and *found* Mary and Joseph and the babe lying in the manger.'

If they had not have *gone* they would not have *found*.

What Biblical theory do we know but are not acting upon?

Matthew 11:28 'Come unto Me all you who are heavy ladened and I will give you rest.'

Proverbs 3:5-6 'Trust in the Lord with ALL ..... ?'

Even if we have never moved from theory we are invited to 'come with haste,' to come quickly, to not delay, NOW is the time to 'Come and Find' His amazing love, compassion and forgiveness.

Maybe our speed of coming has slowed considerably over the years and under the pressures of life. Jesus invites us in Revelation 2:4-5 to return to our first love of Him – to come quickly, not to delay. Now is the time to -

'Come and Find' afresh His amazing love, compassion and forgiveness enabling us to put Him both first and central in our lives day by day.

These were shepherds – they were doing their job – they were looking after sheep who had been put in their care but their expectancy of anything positive happening had faded long ago – whatever their earlier dreams may have been.

Are you / am I a shepherd? Maybe of a large 'flock' or of several 'flocks' or maybe of just one or two sheep? We should all be shepherding some lambs.

If we are honest what is our expectancy level for our 'flock'?

It's not dependant on how good a shepherd we are, or how stubborn or wayward our sheep are, it's far more dependant on our personal level of Adoration and Gratitude to God which will in turn raise our level of Expectancy of what HE is going to do for and with our flock.

How do we view our sheep? As they are, (or as we perceive them to be), or as our wonderful Good Shepherd saw us and sees them – SO worth rescuing and SO full of potential?

Is our expectation
>of / or in the sheep,
>>of / or in ourselves as shepherds
>>>or of /or in the Good Shepherd?

In John15:5 Jesus said "without Me you can do nothing."

But in Matthew 19:26, "with God ALL things are possible."

v12,'And this will be a sign for you, by which you will recognise Him......'

God is SO gracious, not only did he speak so clearly to the shepherds through the angel about the Good News of Great Joy and where to find Him but also how they would know they had got it 'right' - 'this will be a sign for you' - proof that they had followed the instructions correctly even though what they found would be very difficult for them to get their heads around. But yes! Their Saviour, their Messiah, their Lord was, as far as they could understand, going to be a tiny babe, wrapped in swaddling clothes, lying in an animal food trough – well there certainly weren't likely to be many tiny babes lying in mangers in Bethlehem even at this overcrowded time because of the census, but this is who they had to search for.

And as if to encourage them even further to raise their level of Expectation God sends the unearthly / heavenly choir to confirm the angel's message. What must that concert have been like - out on the hills in the dark! I guess it ended as suddenly as it started – they must have been lying on their backs gazing up into the heavens breathless and speechless in awe and wonder. When they did speak v15 they were in NO doubt that it was the LORD – Almighty God – Who had made this Good News of Great Joy known to them, so they chose to 'Go and Find.' They went now with great Expectation whereas an hour before they had no Expectation and were going nowhere.

How ready are we to drop our negativity, our non-expectancy in order to 'Go and Find' what the Lord has already made known to us?

Had they waited for human confirmation Jesus would probably not have been in the food trough in the stable any longer so they would not have known where to look. They would have missed the enormous privilege of being the first to tell others. v17-18

When God reveals things to us He expects us to 'Go and Find' so that we can tell others and they will be astounded and marvel at what we tell them.

Are we willing to receive and act on specific directions from God? The more we obey the ones He has already given us in the Bible the more He is likely to give us His strategies for sharing the

Good News of

Great Joy

wherever He has placed us or sends us.

'Lord please increase my level of positive Expectancy and ready obedience'.

So v16 'they *went*

and *found,*'

and having found, and seen with their own eyes, they shared with all who were there to hear what they had been told about the Child, with the result that all who heard it were astounded and marvelled.

We have no excuse for not sharing what we've heard and seen about Jesus. The shepherds were the lowest of the low, uneducated guys and amazingly it was to them the angels gave the message and confirmation. So without hesitation or inhibitions they spoke out clearly the Good News of Great Joy that they had been given and had now experienced for themselves. This was not pie-in-the-sky theory they were sharing, this was their own experience which no-one could disprove or destroy even if they disputed or disbelieved it. This was their personal testimony and sharing it caused others to marvel and ponder – especially Mary who kept all these things and pondered them in her heart.

Obeying led to sharing, which in turn led others to marvelling, which in turn led to them 'glorifying and praising God for all they had seen and heard just as it had been told them.'

Letting go of their negative expectancy and choosing to take on board what they heard from the angels led to obedience. Until they had 'gone with haste and found' they didn't know if what they'd seen and heard was true or only a figment of their imagination or the result of something they'd eaten for supper, but their obedience led to such an amazing, unexpected privilege of being the first to worship the newly-come-to earth Good Shepherd and King of Kings, and that led them to speak out what they'd been told and that led them to glorify and praise God and to be filled with

A doration

and G ratitude.

Where are we on the shepherd's journey?

Still sitting in the negative expectancy field even having heard the Good News of Great Joy but not attempting to find out if it's true or real?

Or have I gone part way to Bethlehem but not really searched for Jesus?

Or have I arrived at the stable and worshipped but not shared the Great Joy with others?

Or is my daily obedience to what God is asking me to do resulting in a completely new life - full of daily

A doration

G ratitude and

E xpectancy?

No one who really searches for Jesus will be disappointed. He has promised "If you seek Me with all of your heart you will find Me."

So, if we are wise men or shepherds or somewhere in between, whether our Expectancy is, sky-high because of a star, or ground-zero because nothing happens in our lives, or somewhere in between, we all have the option to seek Him, knowing there will be a wonderful outcome which will affect the rest of our lives dramatically if we'll allow it to.

The Holy Spirit longs to work in our hearts and lives and raise our level of Expectancy which will in turn raise our levels of Adoration and Gratitude.

The key is obeying what He – the Almighty God – has already made known to us.

The choice is ours : to stay in the field,

      or to come to the 'food trough' and leave rejoicing.

Which will you / I do today?

The A doration,
The G ratitude,
The E xpectancy of Simeon.

Luke 2 : 25 – 35.

Here was a man full of Expectancy. Presumably a fairly old man but one who knew exactly what he expected before he died.

Why? v26 Because the Holy Spirit had revealed to Simeon that he would not die until he had 'seen the Lord's Christ, the Messiah, the Anointed One.' That was some level of Expectancy to live with.

Why was he given this revelation by the Holy Spirit?

v25 Simeon was a righteous and devout man, cautiously and carefully observing the Divine Law, and looking for the consolation of Israel.

He was looking not just casually, but consistently and carefully observing the Divine Law. He was looking. He was studying. He was longing for the consolation of Israel.

Was he a righteous and devout man – one who undoubtedly adored God – because he consistently and carefully observed the Divine Law or did his righteousness and devotion to God lead him to this careful study? Whichever way round it was, he had God's approval for the Holy Spirit spoke prophetically to him and also prompted him to go to the Temple at the right moment and recognise the right person.

Here was a man who clearly loved God's Word and didn't just know it but carefully observed it and, therefore, did it and sought to understand it at great depth.

He was not a man who was ticking boxes about his standing with Almighty God like many of the religious leaders of the time.

He was a man who was desperate for the consolation of Israel – this was something *far* greater than himself and his family – this was a major heart cry to God for his nation. This was no one-off momentary concern that perhaps things could have been better for Israel. This consumed his soul, his study, his life, his intercession that Israel would know God's consolation whatever that looked like.

What is my level of concern for my nation or any other nation God would lay on my heart?

Is my heart available for Him to lay such a deep heart cry on it?

It will be costly, there is no doubt about that, but the reward - the Holy Spirit revealing secrets about what God will do and giving clear directions as to how He would have me be involved. Surely that is worth any cost isn't it? Or isn't it?

Simeon's was a life of devotion to the Word of God and so to the God of the Word. He was consistently and carefully observing it. Not just picking out the easy bits or the bits he liked but immersing himself in it.

He was looking and longing for the Consolation of Israel – for Israel to be consoled and comforted, exhorted by the tender mercies of Almighty God.

Was his heart and mind in Isaiah 40 where the words so clearly applied to Israel? - v1-2 "Comfort, comfort My people says your God, speak tenderly to the heart of Jerusalem and cry to her that her time of service and her warfare are ended, that her iniquity is pardoned .... v5 and the glory, majesty and splendour of the Lord shall be revealed and all flesh shall see it together for the mouth of the Lord has spoken it........ v9 you who bring good tidings to Zion ......to Jerusalem lift up your voice with strength..... be not afraid, say to the cities of Judah "Behold your God!" v10 Behold your God will come with might and His arm will rule with Him ... His reward is with Him...... v11 He will feed His flock like a shepherd, He will gather the lambs in His arms, He will carry them in His bosom and gently lead those that have their young ...... v28 Have you not heard? The everlasting God, the Lord, the Creator of the ends of the earth, does not faint or grow weary ..... v29 He gives power to the faint and to him who has no might He increases strength ...... causing it to multiply and making it abound.....v31 But those who wait for the Lord – who expect, look for and hope in Him – shall change and renew their strength and power, they shall lift up their wings and mount up close to God as eagles mount up to the sun, they shall run and not be weary, they shall walk and not faint or become tired." Surely this must have been part of the consolation / comfort / exhortation Simeon was looking for so earnestly, longing to see it happen, expecting to see it happen because God had promised him that he would see it before he died.

Did he expect it to be a 40 day old baby? The consolation and comfort and exhortation of Isaiah 40 sounds much more like the most amazing, all powerful, all loving eternal King of kings than a tiny babe, but he was so diligently seeking and expecting to find that he didn't miss God in His amazing camouflage. He knew without any doubt that this was the 'long awaited One.' This was the One who would 'speak comfortably to Jerusalem.' The One who would 'comfort His people.' The One who would care for His sheep and lambs. And because he was so certain about who this wee Babe was he was able to speak over Him prophetically without any doubt or pussyfooting around, and to speak prophetically to Mary as well even difficult, tough words about her future, but spoken in such a way that she was able to receive and ponder them in her heart and not reject them.

Simeon's instant reaction on seeing Jesus was to take Him in his arms – to hold Him close – and to praise and thank God. This was the heart of a person who was used to Adoring and Thanking Almighty God as well as being a man filled with Expectancy. He'd had to wait a long time to see his Expectancy fulfilled but he had obviously been full of:

    A doration and

        G ratitude as well as

            E xpectancy.

How are we in our Adoration and Gratitude when our Expectations don't seem to be being met even though we believe God has promised certain things to us?

Do we know that *our* Expectations are really God-promised or may they just be our wishful thinking?

The more we immerse ourselves in the Word and from there overflow with Adoration and Gratitude the clearer will become our Expectancy.

The A doration
G ratitude
E xpectancy of Anna

Luke 2 : 36 -38.

She must have been at least 104, maybe older, she may have only been 21 when widowed, still in the prime of life, still expecting to be married for many, many years. No doubt she could have remarried – a nearest of kin like Ruth and Boaz – but she must have made a choice – no suitable nearest of kin or that she wanted to give herself completely to God.

What led her to her being a prophetess? She worshipped day and night with prayer and fasting in the Temple.

She was a woman with a passion for God – even still at this great age – she worshipped day and night, presumably she slept in between but this was her life focus. She wouldn't have done this for fun – this was indeed Adoration – ferocious love – loving the Lord with all her mind, her strength, her soul, her body, with her whole being.

Was it any surprise that somewhere along the line she became a prophetess? Someone who is this devoted to God, gives Him so much time and space from a full heart is surely going to be the recipient of God's secrets and be equipped to share them publicly at the right time.

Presumably, like the people she spoke to about Jesus, she too was longing for the redemption / deliverance of Jerusalem. Here she was living in the middle of occupied Jerusalem, in the Temple, longing with all her heart for the Redeemer / Deliverer to come. Had she expected Him to be a 40 day old baby? Most probably not. Had she heard Simeon's proclamation about Jesus? Maybe, but whether or not, she had the witness in her spirit, which was so tuned to hearing God because she spent so much time focused on Him.

Is there any correlation between the depth / reality and length of my worship and the ease, or lack of, my hearing from God?

Do I spend any time really worshipping?

A little time?

A fair amount of time?

Or is it a real priority?

What would I like it to be?

Am I willing to pay the cost?

It may not mean that I have to be a widow or widower for many years or live in a Church but it will mean that I have to talk with God very seriously about my priorities and how He sees them.

What was her response to seeing baby Jesus?

She 'returned thanks to God' and she unashamedly spoke to all who were looking for the redemption of Jerusalem about Him.

What is my response to the Crucified, Risen, Ascended and soon-coming Jesus?

Do I give thanks to God? Do I willingly share what I have found with those who are longing for the same thing – deliverance / redemption? Or do I keep what I believe God has shown me shut away? Do I thank Him for what He has revealed?

A tiny babe, poor parents yet Anna gives thanks to God for the redemption and deliverance of Jerusalem through Jesus. What did she really understand and what redemption and deliverance of Jerusalem did she have in mind as she talked about Jesus to all who were looking for these things?

Has that deliverance / redemption of Jerusalem already come?

It didn't come in her lifetime, or in Jesus' earthly lifetime, Jerusalem was ransacked in AD 70 and the Temple destroyed.

What deliverance and redemption was she speaking of?

Was it at the time of the Balfour Declaration?

Was it at the time of the 6 day war? - June 1967

Or was she speaking about the return of Jesus when HE will come to Jerusalem and rule and reign?

Here was a woman who was listening to the heartbeat of God way ahead of her human time-zone, all because she was absorbed, obsessed with adoring Almighty God with ferocious love that cost her everything. But equally gave her everything that mattered to her as well as longevity.

What cost am I willing to pay to hear so clearly the heartbeat of Father or Jesus?

Dear Holy Spirit please work in my heart and mind that I may develop into a ferocious lover of God?

Anna certainly had great Expectancy about the redemption and deliverance of Jerusalem even though at the time of speaking it was occupied by the Romans. Because of her Adoration which led to her Gratitude - 'She thanked God' - her anticipation was high, even though the fulfilment of that expectancy was to be a long way off. Her belief in it happening was not diminished. She accepted by faith that it would happen. She had prayed for it so much with prayer and fasting day and night. She filled up the bowls – her prayers, like Elisabeth and Zechariah's, had been heard – the answer was there waiting to be released when everything was in alignment that God had in store for that moment in

His – story.

Do I trust God with His timing? Or do I think He's got it wrong? Or do I think He's forgotten? Or do I think that He doesn't care?

Was there a secret / a key to Anna's longevity and her physical and mental well being?

At 104 + she was still focused on her huge amazing God – The one she was sure could, and would, deliver and redeem His people and His land. She didn't just sit there and wait for it to happen, she was pursuing Him day and night. Was this the reason for her mental faculties being intact? She wasn't thinking about herself but about what was on God's heart.

Like Moses, Joshua, Caleb they were all about their Father's business until God took them home with all their faculties intact.

Like my dear friend Judy – who Jesus took home just 2 weeks before her 102 birthday – the older she got the more she pursued God for the salvation of her family, and stood in the gap for Israel and the Middle East, for asylum seekers and refugees, for those being trafficked and for this nation and for many other people and situations that she knew were breaking God's heart but that she equally knew He wanted to bring deliverance and redemption to. Even when she was physically exhausted she would say, 'We must pray for ...' and as she did so she would become physically, vocally stronger.

What is my level of pursuing the heart of God?

Do I want to increase or decrease it?

Am I satisfied with it as it is?

Is God satisfied with it as it is?

God is looking for 'laid down lovers' like Anna.

Am I willing to take that place?

God would love me to, even in my so busy life.

The A doration, G ratitude and E xpectancy of the Wise Men

Matthew 2.

For the Wise Men their Expectancy came before their Adoration and Gratitude.

'We've seen His star in the East and are come to worship Him.'

They *expected* to find the new king, they didn't just hope – they expected.

They so expected that they left home and travelled, maybe for months, just to spend a few minutes with a less than 2 year old in an insignificant town in an insignificant country.

They were so expectant that they prepared gifts to bring with them, this was not just on a whim, on the spur of the moment, 'a let's see what happens' kind of trip.

They set out with real expectancy and it didn't diminish, 'We *have* seen *His* star in the East and are come to worship *Him.*' This was definite! No 'maybe we saw His star in the East and we want to check it out.' They had no doubt that their expectations would be realised / fulfilled.

What journey are we willing to go on to / for God?

What costly preparations are we willing to make?

What time are we willing to give to it?

What is our real level of expectancy?

    a) That it really is of God?

        b) That we do have clear direction?

            c) That we will get to the goal of our journey?

It may not look anything like the challenge / excitement / magnitude of the Wise Men's journey but it may be just as important in God's view and in the effect it has on our lives and the lives of others and also the relevance of what we bring (gold, frankincense and myrrh) to what God is doing at this moment in history

it's - His–Story.

Our level of Expectancy will determine our level of obedience as well as our levels of Adoration and Gratitude.

This was a personal journey the Wise Men took. They didn't send their servants, their representatives, or their friends, they came themselves to where the young Child was. They were willing to pay the personal cost – the taking of the journey, the financial cost of the journey, this was *not* a sponsored camel ride. They were willing to take the risk that all would be well at home while they were away and that they would be safe on the journey which could easily be very hazardous from bandits, wild animals, flash floods and warring tribes etc. Yes, they needed great courage for their journey but their Expectation said

'It's worth it.'

They put their 'everyday' lives, however important, 'on hold' while they went to worship the King of the Jews. They were obviously not Jews, had they been they would have known the Old Testament prophesies concerning the coming Messiah and not have gone to Herod to find out the details.

They came to worship the KING OF THE JEWS. Who do we put our lives on hold for? Is it the King of the Jews or is it to worship a westernised Jesus? Or is it neither?

What difference would it make to our worship and to our attitude if we really realised that Jesus is the King of the Jews? The Wise Men, non-Jews, in Luke 2:2 realised this at the beginning of Jesus' earthly life and Pilate, a non-Jew, in John 19:19 realised it at the end of His earthly life.

For all those 30 plus years in-between, Jesus was the King of the Jews but He was not recognised as such. Mary and probably a few others pondered these things in their hearts through the years with, no doubt, a strange measure of expectation but the Wise Men *knew*.

Their expectation of Adoring the King of the Jews was based on certainty. They knew, that they knew, that they knew that this babe was the King of the Jews.

What difference would it make to us if we worshipped / adored Jesus as the KING of the Jews?

What difference would it make to others in the Church if we worshipped / adored Jesus as the KING of the Jews? Not just the fact that He is *a* Jew but that He is the KING of the Jews.

What difference would it make to our nation if we recognised Jesus as the King of the Jews? How would that change our attitude to the Jews and to Israel?

Jesus is *still* The King of the Jews whatever it looks like politically. Surely this puts a far greater level of Expectation into our praying for Israel and the Jewish people. Even if they don't recognise Him, He has never been de-throned either in Heaven or on earth. Yes, He is the King of the Universe, whatever that looks like, but He is specifically, consistently The King of the Jews and He is a 'good' king. His heart is 200% for His people, that's why He chose to come and chose to die. But He also chose to rise again and re-take His eternal throne – He is indeed King of kings and from that throne He still reigns now as The King of the Jews.

Unlike all other kings there is NO limit to what He can and will do for those who own Him as their King, who worship and Adore, who love with ferocious love this King of the Jews.

Can we sing this old carol and mean the prayer at the end of each verse?

1 As with gladness men of old
Did the guiding star behold,
As with joy they hailed it's light,
Leading onward, beaming bright;
So, most gracious Lord, may we
Evermore be led to Thee.

2 As with joyful steps they sped,
Saviour to Thy lowly bed,
There to bend the knee before
Thee whom heaven and earth adore;
So may we with willing feet
Ever seek Thy mercy seat.

3 As they offered gifts most rare
At Thy cradle rude and bare;
So may we with holy joy,
Pure and free from sin's alloy,
All our costliest treasures bring,
Christ to Thee, our heavenly King.

4 Holy Jesus, every day
Keep us in the narrow way;
And, when earthly things are past
Bring our ransomed souls at last
Where they need no star to guide
Where no clouds Thy glory hide.

Will I worship Him as the King of the Jews or only as my westernised version?

What effect did the Wise Men's Expectancy have on others?

1) Matthew 2:3 'Herod was disturbed and troubled and all Jerusalem with him.' Understandably Herod, a non-Jew, appointed to rule over the Jews was disturbed. Was this new babe going to cause an insurrection in his 'kingdom' which would then get him into deep trouble with the Roman Authority? v4 He was certainly anxious.

2) Strangely the Chief Priests and Scribes – the top Jews of the day – were able to tell Herod and the Wise Men where and when the Christ was to be born. Why weren't they, who were always praying for their Messiah, Redeemer, Liberator to come, already on their way to Bethlehem to worship?

Was it that they had, in their tradition, prayed so long that they had NO level of Expectation?

Was it that in a strange way they were content to be an occupied nation because they, as leaders, had freedom to continue their traditions and if this Child *was* the Messiah it would change *everything* in their lives? They would have to re-think, re-apply everything they knew from the Old Testament. This new born babe was *not* the white-charger-riding Messiah they envisioned.

How easy is it to interpret Scriptures and 'words' that are given to us to fit *our* pictures and ideas, when actually they mean and show something completely different?

Lord help us to really believe Isaiah 55:8;

"For My thoughts are not your thoughts,
neither are your ways My ways, says The Lord."
and help us to open our minds to hear what You
really are saying.

Dare I do that?

v6 The chief priest and scribes quoted to Herod the fact from Micah 5:2 that 'from Bethlehem will come a ruler/leader who will govern and shepherd His people Israel.' Isn't that what they wanted?

Apparently they wanted to continue to govern God's people Israel and shepherd them in a very conscripted manner. They didn't want to loose their control although several times in later years Jesus challenged them.

What difference and effect, if any, does my Expectancy of God really have on others? On those in political authority in the land? On those who seek to constrict the religious practices, not just unbelieving religious leaders, but also those who have completely other agendas, who are seeking to pull down all the loving Commandments that God put in place for the benefit of all mankind?

Does my level of Expectancy have any effect on anyone? Do I want it to have? Does my Expectancy encourage others to be Expectant?

How alive is my Expectancy? Do I really live in the fact that the God whom I declare I worship and believe in, really is The King of kings who is reigning ***now and is Almighty, all-loving etc. etc.*** Is it theory or reality?

The Wise Men's Expectancy was so real, so intense, so overwhelming to them that they determined to make this amazing journey – nothing was going to stop them and so having been to Herod and the chief priests and scribes v9-10 they were thrilled with ecstatic joy when they saw the star again directing them right to the house where Jesus was.

Oh the beautiful humility of these men. v11 'Going in to the house they saw the Child – Jesus – with Mary His mother and they fell and worshipped Him' - there was no fanfare, no trumpet blasts to announce their arrival. The reality of their Expectancy led to immediate worship / Adoration the moment they saw what they had believed for months but until now had not seen.

In John 20:29 AMPC Jesus said to doubting Thomas, 30 years later, "Blessed and happy and to be envied are those who have never seen Me and yet believe and adhered to and trusted in and relied on Me."

The Wise Men had not seen but for the whole of their journey they believed and so when they came to the house the only thing these important, wealthy, strong-minded men could do was fall down on the ground and worship a little toddler. They were not offended that they found Him in a small town, probably in a small house in relative poverty – His stepfather was only a carpenter. They were not offended that they were not wined and dined by the King of the Jews whom they'd made all this effort for.

They were *not* offended.

Am I offended when Jesus doesn't look or behave as I expect Him to?

What is it about Him that offends me? Sometimes? Occasionally? Often?

When we do see Him, in whatever way He appears, what is our instantaneous reaction?

To question? To doubt? Or to worship and adore? To fall down before Him? Or to not worry *at all* about what others think about our response?

v11   They saw and they Adored.

They saw and they Adored.

They saw and they Adored

and *then* they opened their treasure bags and presented their gifts.

What is our order when we meet Jesus? Do we hasten to present our gifts in the hope that they will make us acceptable?

Do we only give part of what we've brought because frankincense and myrrh seem inappropriate for a little toddler?

Do we spend time worrying about how our gifts will be received? Or is our focus *really* on the One to Whom we are giving?

Yes, they came prepared to give – with a heart to give – but their instantaneous giving was Adoration from very full, excited, overwhelmed hearts. Their gifts were very secondary compared with their Adoration even though in the overall scheme of things they were very significant but they probably had no idea of the significance of their gifts apart from the gold, maybe, as they knew He was the KING of the Jews.

When the Holy Spirit prompts us to 'prepare' gifts to bring do we prepare them without question or do we reason in our minds as to whether they are appropriate, whether they will be understood by others? Did Mary and Joseph understand the appropriateness of the gifts? - very doubtful. Maybe we don't understand the relevance ourselves. Does that matter? It may be years - 33 years – before anyone understands the relevance, are we willing to go out on a limb to bring the gifts that God wants?

Am I so immersed in Adoring this amazing God that I *really* forget about myself and concentrate on Him and worship Him with ferocious love? Or do I come into His presence as a child who has made Daddy a special present and all that matters to me is how Daddy likes it, so my worship is actually not Abba-focused, it's me-and-my-gift-focused. This is childish not childlike – we want Abba to adore us, and He does, but at the expense of us not adoring Him?

There are possibly great advantages in coming to Adore our amazing God empty-handed, like the shepherds probably did, because then we won't want to draw attention to ourselves and our lack of gifts but we will be more able to worship / love Mark 12:30 'with all of our heart, with all of our soul, with all of our mind and with all of our strength.' If we have not brought 'gifts' then we will be less distracted from our purpose to worship, to adore, to love with all……

However, there are times when it is very right to bring gifts but our adoration must always take priority over our gifts.

What gifts should we bring? What gifts did the Wise Men bring?

The Gold was fairly obvious because they were bringing presents for a King, but were Frankincense and Myrrh obvious? They were used for sacrifices and embalming. Does one naturally think of taking a healthy toddler the gift of a 'coffin', especially if you expect Him to grow up and reign as King? It would have seemed more appropriate to take Him a beautiful, ornate throne but they didn't.

Gold – A definition:

- is precious, a non-rusting yellow metal;
- is wealth and a source of wealth;
- is brilliant and beautiful;
- is used to make all sorts of things e.g. plates and goblets;
- is used to cover the mundane to produce something splendid e.g. The wooden Pillars in the Temple, were overlaid with gold.

The Wise Men brought what was precious to them and to Jesus. Something which would be permanently precious because it does not rust or deteriorate.

They just opened their treasure bags and gave the gold – their wealth – to the One Who owned everything good and had indeed created everything good including the gold they brought Him.

They just gave it with no strings attached as to how it was to be used or when or if. Did Mary and Joseph use some of it to facilitate their journey into Egypt? Or their stay there as refugees thus easing their situation? Or on their journey back to Nazareth? Or to re-establish the family carpentry business? Or did they just keep it as a very precious gift?

There is no record of the Wise Men checking up years later to see if it had been used wisely. They gave it unconditionally.

If I give my wealth – whatever that may be – the most brilliant, beautiful 'thing' I have, am I content for Him to use it any-which-way or to just keep it hidden but deeply treasured?

My wealth / your wealth may look much more like the young lad's 5 loaves and 2 fishes, John 6:1-14 that's fine if that's what I've got. But the lad didn't tell Jesus what to do with it. He couldn't have had *any* idea what Jesus would do with his lunch. At best he might have thought that he'd given it to Jesus, this dynamic but gentle, captivating teacher, for Him to eat. Never in a million years could he have dreamed of Jesus blessing the gift and breaking it, and breaking it, and breaking it until it fed probably about 15,000 people including the women and children. How mind blowing was that? His little mouth must have been so wide open and his eyes popping out on stalks.

The Secret? He gave without conditions. Jesus could have sent the crowds away hungry and then sat down with just the disciples and shared the lunch – that would have been good, or He could have kept it just for Himself and that would have been such an honour to have Jesus eat your lunch even if you were hungry. But no! When we give what we have, unconditionally, to the One Who has everything there is no limit to what He can do with our gift.

What is my gold?

Am I really willing to give it unconditionally to be used amazingly or simply to be treasured in the heart of the King of kings?

Frankincense – A definition:

> is a white vegetable resin;
> is bitter and glistening;
> is obtained by an incision in the bark of the arbor thuris, the incense tree;
> is used to fumigate at sacrifices; Exodus 30:7
> is used for perfume; Song of Songs 3:6

The gift possibly had little monetary value but it was hugely prophetic and, therefore, highly meaningful.

It was prophetic about the One to whom it was given, not about the givers.

Frankincense was / is white, speaking of Jesus purity.

It is bitter, speaking of what He would have to go through – the garden of Gethsemane, the mock trial, the flogging and the actual crucifixion.

It was obtained by making a gash in the side of the trunk of the tree. Our salvation was obtained through the blood and water that flowed out of Jesus' side when He was pierced.

It was used to fumigate sacrifices – Jesus' death has taken away the stench of our lives, even the stench of what we have offered to God – we are so imperfect that Isaiah 64:6 say that 'all our righteous deeds are like a polluted garment;' they have an awful stench which needs to be neutralised.

It was also used for perfume – having neutralised the stench it filled the vacuum with beautiful perfume.

Oh thank You Jesus for being our Frankincense.

Lord is there any gift that I can bring?

Do I have anything that I can give back to Jesus that speaks so clearly of all that He is and has suffered for me and that covers / neutralises the stench of my life and replaces it with sweet perfume?

Yes! There is the gift of my A doration,

G ratitude,

E xpectancy that He is

my Frankincense.

Myrrh – A definition:

> Is another gum tree resin from a shrubby tree which grows in the Yemen.
> Again the bark is pierced to let it flow out.
> Is variable in colour from pale reddish-yellow to reddish-brown or red;
> Is bitter;
> Is astringent and binding, and stops bleeding;
> Is an antiseptic;
> Is a stimulant;
> Is a drug to assuage pain;
> Is used in perfume;
> Is one of the ingredients used in the anointing oil for the priests;
> Is used for the purification of women;
> Is used for embalming.

It was offered to Jesus when He was on the Cross to alleviate His pain but He refused it in order to retain all His mental faculties to completely fulfil all His Father's will.

But Joseph of Arimathea and Nicodemus would have used it as they took Jesus' body down from the Cross. Yes it was bitter but it would have bound up His wounds – His lacerated back, His side, His head. It would have stopped the bleeding, it was an antiseptic for all these hideous wounds – too late for it to act as a stimulant or to alleviate pain but it would have perfumed His broken body as they anointed and embalmed our everlasting High Priest.

The gifts that the Wise Men brought were a picture of what Jesus is to anyone who will truly worship and adore Him.

He wants to be our Gold :

> our daily provision for all our needs if we use it aright;

> our wealth;

> our brilliance and beauty to be seen by all, as He over-lays us with Himself so that we are hidden but He is seen.

He wants to be our Frankincense :

> and take what is bitter in our lives and turn it into something glittering; and fumigate any sacrifice that we make, even of our best; and perfume our lives so that we become a sweet fragrance that draws people to Him.

He wants to be our Myrrh :

> and be antiseptic in our wounds;

> and stop the bleeding, and bind up our wounds,

> and stimulate us;

> and assuage our pain;

> and anoint us with His perfume;

> and to anoint us to be His Priests;

> and to purify us;

> and to embalm our old nature so that it is really dead.

Maybe the right question to ask is not 'What can / will I give to Jesus?' but

'What am I willing to receive from Jesus and what will I do with it?'

Jesus, You want to be - *my* Gold,

                my Frankincense,

                my Myrrh,

That is amazing!

My real gratitude will be shown by the measure in which I really receive Him in this way.

Equally the measure in which I receive these gifts will determine the size and reality of my consistent

        A doration,

           G ratitude,

              E xpectancy,

That's the gift He loves and longs to receive and He never tires of receiving more and more and more and more.

Lord, surely the story of the gift of the 5 loaves and 2 fishes is a picture of what you did and have continued doing with the gifts from the Wise Men.

You have taken the Gold and blessed it and multiplied it and multiplied it and given it to your disciples down the ages to give to those in financial need.

There has always been enough because you promised that there would be, and You cannot break Your promise, but Lord we your 'now' disciples have not been as careful to obey Your instructions on giving. Your original disciples gave to the hungry and then You instructed them to gather up what remained – there was NO waste, and they ended up with a basket full each. When you blessed and broke it and gave it to the 12 they did not keep it for themselves no matter how hungry they were, they obeyed and then were mightily blessed with a whole basketful each. They showed no signs of greed.

Oh Lord there is so much greed in parts of Your Church. How much it must sadden You because You had compassion on the multitude and they'd only been hungry for 3 days and today there are so many who are long-term hungry and in screaming need even within Your Church.

Holy Spirit please will You show me any areas of greed in my life, whatever form it takes and give me the courage to give away all You don't want me to keep.

It's true that the more we give away the more we will receive and have to enjoy giving away.

You have taken the Frankincense and the Myrrh and multiplied and multiplied them and given them to Your disciples down the ages to use on all who long to be healed, to treat their wounds, to bind up the broken hearted, to purify and to perfume.

Lord, there is always enough of these for ALL of Your children to be using them ALL of the time, whenever, wherever there is a need, with sufficient left over for us also to be blessed, healed and perfumed.

Your whole strategy is one of multiplication.

'Lord will You replace our complacent hearts with Your compassionate heart so that we are willing to be your excited distribution team wherever and whenever You show us there is someone in need.'

From beginning to end of their expedition God spoke to the Wise Men in at least three different ways – probably more but at least three.

God has so many different ways of speaking. How many ways are we willing for God to use to speak to us?

Initially, to these astrologers, He spoke so clearly through something *they,* though very few others were used to. Firstly He spoke through a Star.

Many times God speaks clearly through some aspect of His created universe :

He spoke to Moses through the burning bush,

    to Noah through the rainbow,

        to Abram through the stars and sand,

            to the Israelites through the cloud and fire

- phenomena that were natural and yet in these instances were clearly 'supernatural' and so packed with an intensity which spoke so clearly to the people concerned.

How do we / do I view the created universe? As something to be enjoyed and which I can appreciate, which often makes me feel 'good?' It may even cause me to exclaim at the beauty of a sunset but do I expect God to speak some new clear message through His creation directly to me?

Many times He has brought assurance / confirmation to me that He is in control, that I'm on the right path etc. through a very timely stunning rainbow, but I can't call to remembrance receiving a clear directive or new piece of knowledge in this way.

Then God spoke to them through the religious leaders who directed them to what the Old Testament said, even though they themselves were not believing it or responding to it. God's Word IS God's Word, no matter who it is spoken by it can still work in the hearts and lives of the hearers even if the speakers don't believe or understand it. How precious is that? That in every Church, every service where the Word is read it can bear fruit in the lives of the hearers.

Thank you Lord for the time you spoke to me so clearly at a 'united' service on a Pentecost Sunday evening through the reading of Exodus 31 (The account of God filling Bezalel and Oholiab with His Spirit to do all the work of making the Tabernacle) even though the preacher said, 'I know nothing about the filling of the Holy Spirit or whatever this story is all about,' But You used that reading of the Scriptures by a man who humbly admitted that he didn't understand, to answer the question I had already been asking You - 'Was I really doing what You wanted me to be doing?' which happened to be working in Judith's wool shop, especially creating / making one off fashion knitwear as well as serving and being there for customers. As clear as a bell that passage confirmed Your calling on my life for the next 10 – 11 years even though it was read and talked about by a man who openly admitted that this was way outside his experience.

…..BUT GOD….. and HIS WORD

are not limited in any way by who is reading it out loud, the limitation is in the mind / heart of the hearers if there is one.

How prejudiced am I by who is reading / preaching The Word?

To what extent is my level of Expectancy re hearing from God through the spoken Word dependent on my assessment of the person speaking audibly and not on the One Who is really speaking it – The Living Word?

And then in Matthew 2:12 in answer to their specific question about whether to return to Herod or not, so important that they asked the question and didn't just conform to etiquette or presume, and so did not succumb to the sin of presumption. We don't know if the 'different way' was easier or harder but whichever they willing went by a new, unknown route as God directed them because they asked. God spoke to them through a dream -'they were *divinely* instructed and warned in a dream not to go back to Herod.'

Did each of the Wise Men have the same dream or just one of them and the others witness to it's validity? We don't know. What we do know is that by obeying this dream it gave Joseph time to flee from Israel with Jesus and Mary before Herod could assassinate the real King of the Jews.

In so many countries around the world today, where there is little or no freedom to read or teach the Word, God is speaking to 1,000s of people through dreams, introducing Himself to them individually, personally and 1,000s are becoming believers every day.

They are being 'Divinely Introduced and Instructed.'

How choosy are am I as to how God should speak to me or to anyone else?

Wise men and women and young people and children still seek Jesus, not just at Christmas but right throughout their lives. Nothing is more important. Nothing is more fulfilling. Nothing is more exhilarating.

This is not a casual seeking, this is if you 'seek Me with ALL your heart you will be found of Me' Deuteronomy 4:29, Jeremiah 29:13. And the result will be that the more we seek Him the more we will find / come to know Him and the easier it will be to fall at His feet in adoration and the greater our Adoration the greater will be our Gratitude. And the greater our Gratitude the greater will be our Expectation of seeing His glory manifest in the darkest places of this world that He loves SO much and indeed in the darkest places, in the smallest places, in the insignificant places of our lives too.

The Wise Men's Expectancy was purely to be able to Worship the King of the Jews. There was no expectancy about what He would do for them or that they would be used in any special way.

Is my Expectancy / Worship that pure?

Holy Spirit please show me if / where my Expectancy and Adoration come with strings attached and so is not pure.

Every day we can receive Jesus' gifts of - Gold

- Frankincense

- Myrrh

Every day we can give Jesus our gifts of - A doration

- G ratitude

- E xpectation.

He would so love us to both receive and give.

That will give Him SO much joy

Will we do that?

Epilogue

Hello dear reader, dear fellow traveller I hope that you have been blessed by journeying with these precious characters in the Christmas narrative.

So what now that you've finished the book?

We have choices:

You can just put it back on the shelf or you can 'grow' it.

How do we grow it?   There are several possible ways :

1) We can go back to the 1st section - 'Adoration' and think of other aspects of God that cause us to adore Him and write another or several other sections 'God You are ……. and I adore You for it.'

2) We can go to the 2nd section - 'Gratitude' and add things to the list that we are personally grateful to God for. 'God You have ….. and I'm so grateful.' 'I'm so grateful that You are my …..'

Have 'fun' writing another 'chapter or chapters'.

3) We can go to the list of things in 'Gratitude' that have been part of our lives in the past but God has saved us out of or we recognise that there are still things - characteristics - which we need to be save out of and established into the opposite Christ-like characteristic. Spend time there asking the Holy Spirit to show you what His assessment is and what He still longs to save you out of and translate you into. There may be other characteristics you need to add to the list. Then let's

commit to working with the dear Holy Spirit for these transformations to grow in our lives.

4) You may want to go to the character biographies and see who you feel most 'at home with' be it the shepherds with initially no adoration, no gratitude, and no expectation or like Elisabeth and Zechariah with much Adoration and Gratitude but no Expectation, or any of the others and ask the Holy Spirit to show you where He would like you to enjoy an 'upgrade' in any or all of these qualities that Jesus would so like you to minister to Him everyday and not just at Christmas.

So if you want to get the most out of this wee book then please don't just put it on the shelf but 'grow it' and make it your own.

His answer to the question -

> 'What
> > Would
> > > He
> > > > Like
> > > > > For
> > > > > > Christmas?'

Is still the same:

> "I would love your A doration,
>
> > your G ratitude &
> >
> > > your E xpectancy."

Let's bring Him much joy every day as He gives us breath,

and not just at Christmas.

and now dear friend :

'May the grace and joyous favour of the Lord Jesus Christ, the unambiguous love of God and the precious communion that we share in the Holy Spirit be yours continually.'
1 Corinthians 13:14.

'May grace and perfect peace cascade over you as you live in the rich knowledge of God and of Jesus our Lord.'
2 Peter 1:2.

www.ingramcontent.com/pod-product-compliance
Lightning Source LLC
Chambersburg PA
CBHW061231070526
44584CB00030B/4077